PRAISE FOR *INTENTIONALITY FOR LEADERS*

"I love this book. I use the term love intentionally. I can tell I love it because I want to keep reading. That's something I've never said about any other book on leadership. The lessons are well illustrated using relatable examples. The science presented herein is accurate. It's a very quotable book. Thank you for putting such a useful tool out there, Herb."

DAN EDGAR, Ph.D., Consulting Psychologist, Nova Scotia, Canada

"As a colleague, I had the honor of observing as Herb took to his clients his message of intentionality and the idea that talk, goals, and plans are simply not enough. Herb helped those clients understand that intentionality was the missing piece that was keeping them from achieving their highest aspirations. All the life and organizational change ideas Herb brought to his clients are captured in this book. As I read each chapter, I began making a list of clients and business associates that would benefit from and thoroughly enjoy reading this book. Having read all the books that Herb references and 100s more, I can candidly say this book now ranks in my all-time top ten. I highly recommend that you read it once all the way through and then go back and read one chapter at a time and work through the questions, concepts, and models before proceeding to the next chapter. Fantastic job sharing your insight and personal journey with the world. Five stars!"

MIKE MARSHALL, Executive Coach, Successamplified.com, Louisville, KY

"Excellent is all I can say. This book is a summary of everything Herb has taught me over the years and a great reference for me to go back to when I lose sight of what I need to be doing! It's his brain in a book LOL!!

Having had the pleasure and honor of Herb's coaching to help my team and me over the course of a decade, I can truly say he has had one of the biggest impacts on my professional career and personal life. Shortly after earning "my shot" to be the GM at a car dealership, I met Herb through Ford's Consumer Experience Movement. I knew I had a foundation of leadership, and Herb coached me into becoming the leader I am today. I am truly grateful for his commitment to me and my team and the friendship we have developed over the years."

GREG KIMBALL, General Manager, Maxwell Ford, Group 1 Automotive, Austin, TX (Top 25 Ford dealer in the nation)

"My team and I have had the privilege of working with Herb for almost a decade. We have taken many deep dives through the topics illustrated in this book. Simple changes in perspective have helped shape me and my team to create amazing results. It has been a great gift to have Herb and the perspectives he shares in this book be a part of our journey. Ultimately, success is a decision (or series of decisions) along with appropriate action. We have learned that some things come naturally; for everything else, you need intentionality. Thank you to my friend and *brother* Herb."

MIKE RENTFRO, General Manager, College Station Ford, College Station, TX

"I must say, well done! We share a similar passion for living an intentional life, and the world needs more Herb Mast thinking. This book offers a transformative perspective on the power of awareness and intentionality, guiding readers to overcome ignorance and embrace growth. By emphasizing the value of candid feedback, transparent relationships, and purposeful actions, it equips individuals to unlock their potential and achieve meaningful personal and professional development."

JUSTIN QUIGLEY, Founder and CEO, Fresh Talent

"This methodology, from formulating Intentionality Steps to the recruitment and engagement of a winning team, to the ultimate task of coaching and forging that team into the best versions of themselves for the benefit of those around them, has obvious relevance to the business arena but transcends into the realm of family and social relationships just as elegantly. Whether responsible for a staff of 5 or 500, Herb Mast has illustrated that the practice of intentionality is transformative as we all grow in leadership. At Bozard Ford-Lincoln, we treat Herb's work as a foundational element of our leadership development curriculum. The efficacy of the principles outlined in *Intentionality for Leaders* has played a key role in creating a positive, motivated, and aligned staff that has grown our dealership into one of the 10 highest-selling Ford franchises in the country."

BO BOZARD, CEO, Bozard Ford Lincoln, St. Augustine, FL
(Top 10 Ford Dealer in the nation)

"Herb Mast has helped so many clients achieve success through greater intentionality. And now he has put it into a book. This is a soup-to-nuts approach to both leadership and achievement. It is dense with practical insight for anybody who would actually like to *accomplish* something. Highly recommended."

MARK HARRISON RAMSAY, Founder, Hip Socket,
Berea, KY

"As I read Herb's book, the lightbulb in my head turned on. The concept of intentionality in authoritative leadership and organizational success was the switch that lit the bulb. Herb, in a clear and understandable manner, explores the topic of intentionality. In addition, he provides real-time examples, models, and guidance for any leader to incorporate intentionality into one's personal leadership strategy. This is a very good read and a call to action for leaders at any stage of one's career."

DR. JAMES KIRCHNER, President, Global Assist.
Former President SynergEyes.

“There are a lot of books on leadership. What separates this book is how Herb takes the best leadership concepts and simplifies them into real-world applications. There is nothing easy about being a leader, but for those up to the challenge, this book is your blueprint on how to create and grow a successful team and organization.”

PATRICK CHASTANG, COO, Chastang Auto Group,
Houston, TX

“If you are looking for a book that will help you transform your leadership style and your organization, I highly recommend *Intentionality for Leaders* by Herb Mast. This book is not just a collection of theories and concepts, but a practical guide that shows you how to apply the principles of intentionality to your everyday challenges and opportunities. Intentionality is the ability to act with purpose, clarity, and focus, and to align your actions with your values and vision. It is the key to becoming a great leader, who can inspire others, create a positive culture, and achieve remarkable results.”

I can personally attest to the power of intentionality, as I have been working with Herb Mast as my leadership coach for over 10 years. He has helped me and my 4th-generation family business to develop a clear vision of where we want to go as a company and to establish core values that define who we are… what behavior we will tolerate as a company and what behavior we simply will not stand for. He has also helped us to overcome the “Crazy Quilt” of competing agendas that used to plague our organization and to foster a strong and confident team that leads with our heads and our hearts. Thanks to Herb’s guidance and support, we have improved our communication, collaboration, and performance, and we have become more resilient, profitable, and adaptable in the face of change.

Intentionality for Leaders is not just a book, but a journey that will challenge you, inspire you, and empower you to become the best leader you can be. Whether you are leading a small team or a large organization, this book will provide you with the tools, strategies, and insights you need to practice intentionality in every aspect of your leadership.

If you are ready to take your leadership to the next level, I urge you to read *Intentionality for Leaders* by Herb Mast. It will change your life and your organization for the better."

BRADFORD H. RANDALL, Dealer Principal, Randall Ford, Fort Smith, AR

"I have had the opportunity to converse and work with Herb over the last many years. I consider him a friend who practices what he preaches through intentionality. This book again brings to life the many hours of coaching and development he has given me and our organization as we strive to grow and develop. *Intentionality for Leaders* is a simple, but not easy, take on what creates success in leadership."

STEPHEN LIVESAY, COO Keating Auto Group, Victoria, TX, Auto Group with 28 stores.

"A simple guide to the undeniable truths about great leadership. Explained in a manner that captivates its audience and gives them the real tools necessary to become a great leader."

DUSTIN KRIEGER, General Manager, Cedar Park Nissan, Cedar Park, TX

"I have known Herb for over 20 years. God has blessed Herb with incredible talents to create, coach, and inspire others. These talents are naturally displayed throughout this book. His ability to diagnose the root issues and present models and solutions to the everyday challenges of life we all face is a refreshing approach that creates real results. Herb lives with intentionality, and it has become part of his DNA. It is a way of life in how he lives and serves others. He describes intentionality as being purposeful and deliberate in our actions to optimize positive results and minimize negative ones. When we take purposeful action that is in alignment with our values and philosophies, we not only change personally, but we also begin to change the world around us.

This book is packed with what we need to assess and engage life with intentionality. The models and methods Herb shows us lead us on a path of discovery and ultimately to a point of decision.

Herb reminds us that leaders do not force others to follow; they invite them on a journey. When you begin reading and applying these teachings, you will begin a new journey of intentionality to create positive results that last a lifetime. A journey that will impact all areas of your life."

BARRY LOCKHARD, President and CEO, Cornhusker Bank, Lincoln, NE

"I wholeheartedly endorse *Intentionality for Leaders* by Herb Mast. Having worked alongside Herb for three years, I've witnessed firsthand his unwavering commitment to leading with intentionality. In this insightful book, Herb distills his years of experience and wisdom into practical guidance that will empower leaders at all levels to navigate their journeys with purpose and authenticity."

JEFF KING, Vice President and General Manager, Bozard Ford Lincoln, St. Augustine, FL (Top 10 Ford Dealer in the nation)

"As someone who has always had good intentions but struggled to complete them, *Intentionality for Leaders* helps me understand the why and how. It gives me a process to have greater intentionality in both my business and personal life."

PHILIP WEIKERT, General Manager, Weikert Ford, Lake Wales, FL

"In his new book, *Intentionality for Leaders*, Herb Mast has brought together the great teachings on leadership and combined them into his proven application method that will fundamentally and permanently impact the processes, communication, and performance of your team!"

DEREK LEE, General Manager, Long McArthur Ford, Salina, KS

"Herb Mast is a grassroots leader's leader. I've seen him in action as a business coach in the automotive industry, and there just aren't any better. On a 1-10 scale, I'd give him a 9.7. I'd give him a 10, but then he might relax and not write another great book like this one. Mr. Mast is an all-or-nothing kind of guy and he'll want that 10 - intentionality in action. Great read, sound advice, and I guarantee it came from the heart of a man who knows how to get things done."

BRUCE ARMES, Good Reviews Plus, LLC, Florida

"The writer Annie Dillard once said - *"How we spend our days is, of course, how we spend our lives. What we do with this hour, and that one, is what we are doing."*

It isn't difficult to see how this might apply to the culture we create within our businesses.

She also said - *"Assume you write for an audience consisting solely of terminal patients."*

In a manner of speaking, all customers are 'terminal'. Or, at least transient. There is no guarantee they will be here tomorrow.

Which is why the message Herb Mast presents us with in this exciting compendium is both critical and urgent - *The importance of Intentionality.*

'Intentionality' is only a degree or two away from the word... *'intensity'*. It is a word that has worked its way to us from the Old French *'entencioun'* and before that from the Latin *'Intentionem'*, which means *"stretching out, straining, exertion, effort, and attention."*

'In' means *"toward"* and *'tendre'* means *"stretch..."* like a tendon.

But *'stretch toward'* what? That which you wish to see come true. It might be a dream, a specific goal, increased capacity, or agility. But without *'intentionality'*, we find ourselves adrift and vulnerable to the random cross-currents of life's daily chaotic and unfocused predicaments. We find ourselves constantly derailed, set back, and gradually de-energized.

In these pages, Herb Mast unfolds a careful and structured approach for returning control to ourselves in a way that both invites and cultivates creative intelligence, as well as holds our feet to the fire of practical and realistic application.

This is a compendium built on years of *'intense'* front-line line field-experience, chronicling and drawing from the latest and evolving science of human behavior, leadership intelligence, and best practices for playing at a higher level and achieving extraordinary performance."

JOHN KUZAVA, Culture & Transformation Strategist,
Keynote Speaker. Strategy & Design Director,
Ford Consumer Experience Movement
2010 – 2018, Michigan

"I have witnessed firsthand Herb's commitment to the tenets of his book and the success it has brought him. A great read for leaders and those looking to improve."

DAVID DARLINGTON, Wealth Management Advisor,
Northwestern Mutual

INTENTIONALITY FOR LEADERS

INTENTIONALITY FOR LEADERS

BEYOND MERE TALK,
ACTIONLESS GOAL SETTING,
AND GOOD INTENTIONS
TO REAL AND SUSTAINABLE RESULTS

HERB MAST

Printed in the United States of America.

I dedicate this book to my wife, my best friend and life partner, who has supported me in all my many endeavors for more than 40 years. Together, we have discovered the value of living with intentionality, which has not only defined us individually and as a couple, but ever increasingly strengthened our relationship.

TABLE OF CONTENTS

In all toil there is profit, but mere talk tends only to poverty.

- PROVERBS 14:23

Some things come natural, for everything else you need intentionality.

– MIKE RENTFRO

FOREWORD

When Herb asked me to write the forward for his book, Intentionality for Leaders, I was honored. When Mindy Holman agreed to write the forward to my book Be the Sun, not the Salt, I was thrilled, and when I read what she wrote, it made me weep. Unfortunately, I now have that as my standard. I want Herb to weep when he reads this. I know that's an unrealistic expectation, but why not have high standards? I met Herb while I was consulting with Ford Motor Company, and he was one of the coaches assigned to help automotive dealerships bring out the best in their people. I worked with many coaches, consultants, and facilitators over my many years in the business, and Herb stands out among them as one of those people who was as hungry to learn as he was hungry to teach. Most good coaches want the best for their clients, but Herb has gone one step further. He has packaged his years of collected wisdom into this book so that, when he leaves this earth, he has left his clients a useful handbook to use long after he is gone. I can hear the passion in the words written on these pages because I know him. If you don't know him, the wisdom he has collected in this book will still serve anyone interested in helping their teams and organizations thrive. The general manager of one of the dealerships he currently serves (an already high performance organization) told me that Herb has truly helped them achieve new levels of excellence in their personal and professional lives and continues to do so with every single monthly visit year after year after year. His work has helped them and countless others. What more could anyone ask of one's life? Herb, please know that you made a positive difference in the lives of many. I hope this book does the same.

Harry D. Cohen PhD
Harry.Cohen@Holman.com
http://bethesunnotthesalt.com

BACKSTORY

My late father-in-law shared a riddle with me many years ago. He said, "There were three frogs on a log. One decided to jump off. How many frogs were left on the log?"

It's not a trick question, and the math is quite simple.

State your answer out loud before reading further.

Most people answer two, but two is not correct.

As you scratch your head and re-read the question to try to discover where you went wrong, let me give you a hint— deciding to do something is not the same as actually doing it.

Want to change your answer?

Here's the point: Regardless of whether a frog decides to jump off or not, all three frogs remain on the log until one or more actually jump. So, the right answer to the riddle is three.

The frog's decision to jump does not necessarily or automatically translate into the action of jumping. Intentions are simply thoughts.

Intentionality, on the other hand, by definition, involves action. Intentional action. Not just random action, but purposeful and deliberate action.

Many try to argue this is just semantics. I disagree. Words matter. More importantly, actions matter. And therein lies the challenge for most people and explains why most don't achieve more of the things they want. A plan without action is just an idea or dream. People may have many thoughts and make many statements of things they plan or intend to do, usually with good intentions, but all too often, they do not follow through with action.

A couple of examples might help clarify and provide initial insight into why the practice of intentionality is so important to understand and embrace if you want to achieve more of the things that are important to you.

Intentionality example one: Imagine a person (we'll call her Jill) is asked by a coworker if she will help serve dinner at a local homeless shelter for Thanksgiving.

Partially in the pressure of the moment, and partially because Jill is ultimately a good person with good intentions, she agrees to the request. However, when the day of the event comes, Jill doesn't show up. Why she doesn't show up is irrelevant at this point. She may have reasons that make sense to her, but the issue is that she doesn't show, even though she said she would. It might be helpful to know that this isn't the first time Jill has made a commitment and not followed through. Not following through seems to be a pattern for her and is partially attributable to her personality.

The dinner proceeds, but the team serving the meal is short-handed. Jill not showing up, especially without notice, causes others to scramble to fill the void and requires everyone else to work harder.

The consequences of Jill's lack of action, in not showing up, are probably small in this situation, although this pattern applied to other situations could be significant. There are instances every day where people have good intentions and make commitments but don't follow through. Being late to work is similar. And every time, whether small or large, there are consequences, intended or not, for us or others, directly or indirectly for unfulfilled commitments.

So, why did Jill say she would do it if she wasn't committed to following through? Most likely, Jill originally fully intended to participate, but when the time came, she either forgot or had something else she wanted or had to do.

Jill's lack of intentionality in this instance is an example of inaction, which is one of the two greatest achievement killers.

Not surprisingly, many people do exactly what Jill did: make a potentially flippant commitment with little regard for their ability or desire to follow through. This represents a good intention, which gives a momentary good feeling—volunteering for a good cause. It also provided immediate, albeit temporary, relief from the moral pressure of the moment—facing a request to participate or donate.

Many people commit to things simply to get out of awkward situations—face-to-face requests—with little consideration for what they committed to do. Unfortunately, and the reality is that, there are always consequences. In this case, the consequence for the team was working short-handed. Jill's reputation was also negatively impacted. And from a personal perspective, at some point, Jill will no doubt suffer emotional distress, knowing she let others down with her inaction.

When broken promises become a pattern in a person's life, it's easy to understand why it's said that the road to hell is paved with good intentions. Unfulfilled commitments invariably result in negative consequences for somebody, if not everybody, including us.

Intentionality example two: A father (we'll call him Jack] is working hard to build his career. He's enjoying success through higher wages and promotions but at the cost of less time with his family. Even though the family also benefits from the lifestyle that Jack's hard work affords, they miss having him around and involved with the family. Jack feels this pressure and makes hollow promises to appease his family's expectations.

Periodically, his spouse and/or children make reasonable requests that require Jack's time. Being distracted by other pressures, not having the immediate time available, and wanting to avoid potential conflict and disappointment, Jack promises to do what they want, but at some point in the future, rather than now. While his promise buys him time now, it also creates a debt or obligation that his family expects to collect on in the future. These deferred commitments are like using credit cards to pay for goods that we don't have the money for today. The credit card balance increases and will have to be paid at some point.

Imagine the classic scenario where Jack promises to take his son fishing on the weekend. But, when the weekend comes, Jack breaks his promise, because some things came up at work that he needs to take care of. So he promises his son to take him the following weekend.

Just like in Jill's case, Jack makes a promise in the moment, with good intent and to avoid immediate conflict. What Jack doesn't fully consider, however, is how his momentary relief through deferring his promise creates an even greater future obligation. Again, this is like credit cards. It's easy to use them in the moment, but eventually, they will need to be paid, often with added interest.

Each time Jack breaks his promise, his son's expectations go up, in offset of his growing disappointment. At the same time, the son's trust in his father's word is eroded.

Intentionality is about action—intentional and deliberate action—not just words.

Words are helpful in expressing intent, but ultimately, words are meaningless without action. The bible says that it's better not to make a promise yet do something than to make a promise and not follow through (Matthew 21:29-31).

So, what is intentionality, and how does it lead to greater achievement?

Intentionality is defined as intentional or purposeful action—doing things on purpose. While intentionality can represent a single purposeful action, when it comes to life and leadership, intentionality represents many small actions directed by a philosophy and leading to consistent behaviors or a lifestyle, which allow an individual or organization to achieve more of what they want—usually delineated in mission, vision, and values statements.

Here's an example of an organization that exemplifies intentionality and achieves superior results.

Chick-fil-A is a well-known and highly regarded American fast food restaurant chain, based in Hapeville, Georgia, a suburb of Atlanta, that specializes in chicken sandwiches. Founded in 1946 by Truett Cathy, the Chick-fil-A team operates more than 2,300 restaurants in 47 states (2019 data) and is the most profitable fast-food restaurant amongst its competitors, even though they are only open six days a week [closed Sundays] where their competitors are open seven.

I had the opportunity to go behind-the-scenes and tour their Support Center [Corporate Headquarters] in the fall of 2019 to learn some of the keys to their success.

During the tour, I learned how the organization practices intentionality in building a high-impact and consistent culture. Everything, as explained during the tour, is done with intentionality—their values, their processes, their meetings, their marketing, etc., and even the tour.

They repeatedly used the word intentional when referring to how they design and do things, but more importantly in describing how they follow through with deliberate and consistent action to create a quality product and a consistently superior customer experience.

A few examples of the intentionality of their words:

- In their restaurants, as in the rest of the organization, they say, "My pleasure," rather than, "You're welcome." The inference is that it is their pleasure to serve, not just to complete a transaction.
- They do not have customers, but rather guests.
- They do not have employees, but rather team-members.
- Their Home Office is referred to as a support center, not Corporate, recognizing that the home office's most important function is to serve the needs of their team-members so they can better serve guests.

Again, this is not simply semantics—Guest, Team-Member, Support Center, and "My pleasure" serve to align the team with the organization's vision, goals, and values. The words guide action with great intention. The intentional and consistent use of specific words embed the values and guiding principles of the organization into every aspect of operations to remind team members of not only how they should behave, but why it's important to behave a certain way.

When team-members don't operate in line with these guiding principles, appropriate [positive but resolved] conversations take place. Team-members either choose to align with the culture of the organization or leave. Tolerating incongruent behavior would dilute, and ultimately destroy, Chick-fil-A's culture and lead to lower performance.

Being aligned around a common purpose is critical for an organization, regardless of what business it's in. Having alignment conversations is necessary whenever words are used or behaviors are observed that do not align with the values of the organization.

Alignment is critical to the effective and efficient operation of any organization. Unfortunately, too many leaders ignore the signs of misalignment or choose to avoid conflict. The adverse consequences of inaction can be significant and even fatal to the brand.

A good question to ask at times of potential misalignment is, "Don't know, don't care, or can't?" In other words, does the individual not know what the expected behaviors are, do they not care, or are they incapable of the behavior?

The responsibility of leaders is to educate and train people who don't know. But, if they have done their job of providing clarity and training, the only remaining explanation is that the misaligned team member either doesn't care or can't. Both latter conditions should disqualify the person from being on the team.

Having the courage to engage in alignment conversations is a defining characteristic of an intentionality-based leader.

Intentionality-based leadership is foundational to the effective functioning of teams and to the achievement of superior outcomes.

This book is devoted to developing great leaders, who produce superior results by practicing intentionality.

This book consists of four sections:

1. Foundational Principles and Concepts
2. The Intentionality Model
3. The Intentionality Formula
4. The Three Intentionalities of Great Leaders

My desire is that this book will not only help you understand the art and science of intentionality, but that in the process of practicing intentionality, you will achieve more of the things that are important to you, your team, and the organization you have the privilege of leading.

THE DISCOVERY

The greatest obstacle to discovery is not ignorance—it is the illusion of knowledge.

— DANIEL J. BOORSTIN

I distinctly remember exactly where I was when I first started referring to the concept of intentionality.

I was standing in front of the leadership team in a client's conference room, sharing ways to achieve more as a team, when I wrote the word intentionality on the whiteboard. I remember pausing for a moment and questioning aloud whether this new word was even a word.

Those of you who conduct seminars and workshops know that all kinds of interesting things happen when using whiteboards. One thing is for sure, spelling goes out the window with whiteboards. I don't know what it is about a whiteboard, but in the moment, it seems the simplest of words are easily misspelled when writing them on a whiteboard.

I proceeded to share with the team principles and concepts that would help them better achieve their goals. These principles and concepts have been refined over more than ten years as I have worked with dozens of clients as a Leadership Coach and are now presented in this book.

Before getting into the details of the principles and concepts, let me share with you two stories that demonstrate the power of intentionality in my own life.

The first story starts in my garage on February 5, 2011, and unfolds over a period of a few months.

We had two of our grandchildren visiting for the day. Before proceeding further, in case you're thinking this guy must be really old, I should point out that both my wife and I and our oldest son and his wife had children by the time we were twenty-three, so we were grandparents by the time we were forty-six.

My wife and I would periodically have our grandkids stay over on a Friday night, giving their parents a date night and a chance to sleep in on Saturday. In this case, we had recently moved into our new house, and we were still unpacking a few boxes.

I have the blessing [and curse] of being an achiever. I'm not boasting. Achiever is a trait or talent that can be discovered through various assessments, like the Gallup® StrengthsFinder assessment, which showed Achiever as my top talent theme out of thirty-four themes. I also know this intuitively, as it's hard for me to go through a day and not get something accomplished.

It's a blessing because I'm driven to get lots done. I have a high propensity for work. It served me well through my entrepreneurial years, but on this particular Saturday, it proved to be a curse.

After a morning of playing with the grandkids (Lukka was four, and Annika was two), it was time for their nap. The disorganization in the garage was bothering me, and their naptime gave me an opportunity to spend time in the garage organizing and building shelves.

It was not long into nap time that I had an accident while hoisting a 4x8 sheet of ¾" plywood above my head while climbing a 6' stepladder. The goal was to slide the sheet into two rails I had installed above the garage door. Lifting of the sheet was not the difficult part. Rather, climbing the steps with the sheet above my head while maneuvering the sheet into place proved a little challenging.

It was about the time that I scaled the 4th step that I realized how wobbly the stepladder was. Within short order, I found the ladder going left and the plywood going right. There was not much time to think, but within a split second, I had the idea come to me to try to pinch the plywood against the wall, which was only about three feet to my right. I'm not sure now whether my plan would help me save myself, the plywood, or both. This was no ordinary sheet of plywood; this was a quality sheet of fine birch. Granted, it only cost about forty-five dollars, but sometimes, we don't think our best when we are falling off a ladder.

I'm confident that my plan also included easing my fall somehow, but everything happened so quickly.

It's relevant to mention that, at this stage of my life, I weighed 220 pounds, which is a lot for my five-foot-seven-and-a-half-inch frame. Needless to say, the board and I both fell to the ground with a loud crash, which my wife heard from inside the house.

As I picked myself off the floor, I immediately noticed that my right wrist had an odd shape. It was obvious that I had broken my wrist and arm. The orthopedic surgeon would later advise me that this was the second worst break he had seen in thirteen years. It wasn't just broken; my wrist was shattered. Further, it was a compound fracture—that's the kind where a bone punctures through the skin.

As a testament to American healthcare, I was in surgery within three and a half hours of the accident. Afterwards, the PA (Physician's Assistant) shared with me that most compound breaks involve about a ninety-minute surgical procedure; the break, however, was so severe that after about an hour into the surgery and assessing the damage, the surgeon was not sure how best to proceed. The PA later told me that he suggested an approach that would utilize external traction to hold things in place as best as possible until the bones healed and then deal with future mobility issues during rehab, which I learned would have been a long and difficult process.

I'm thankful to the surgeon for the course of treatment that he chose. His practice involved dealing with many student athletes from the local University, and I'm going to assume his past experiences with athletes influenced his decision. He utilized a steel plate and eight screws to hold the biggest pieces together, all of which are still in my arm to this date. Because of this, I never really had a cast. I had a half cast that fit around the side of my wrist and a roll of elastic bandage that held it in place.

As I sat in my hospital room the next morning, the surgeon explained the seriousness of my injuries and what he had done to stabilize the bones. As he told me about the rehab process, all I could think about was golf. I had become addicted to the sport (golfers know what I mean; others will be confused at this point) and asked the surgeon whether I would ever be able to play golf again—this was around the time that he took hold of my bloodied and curled up fingers and straightened them. I'm not sure I had ever felt pain like that before. Not even the actual fall from the ladder and initial break hurt that bad—to which he replied, "That's up to you."

For an achievement-oriented person, that is all I needed to hear. In follow-up visits, the PA and surgeon showed me how to rehab my wrist and told me to let pain be my guide. In the ensuing days, I followed the doctor's instructions and worked at rehabbing my wrist. I was very intentional with my rehab efforts, such that, within two weeks, I was able to hold a golf club. Within four weeks, I was able to start swinging the club. And, after six weeks, I was able to play my first round. It was not a pretty round, but I scored under 100 and was excited to be playing.

I was not thinking about intentionality at this point, because I had not "discovered" it yet, but I was certainly practicing it. Rehab involved a consistent and continual process of little actions, including lots of stretching, while using pain as my guide of how far to push myself.

I have continued to play lots of golf since then and am pleased to report that I have been able to become an even better golfer, not because of the accident, but despite it, by practicing intentionality.

The second story takes place over a period of eight months, from December 31, 2011 to July 28, 2012.

At the time, I weighed approximately 220 lbs. Not bad for somebody who is 6' 4". The problem is I am not 6' 4". I was at the time 5' 7.5".

There are a few times each year when we give ourselves license to indulge, like our birthdays and anniversaries. But the trifecta takes place at the end of each year: Thanksgiving, Christmas, and New Year's. Well, that indulgence, together with the busyness and stress of life, resulted in me gaining 50 pounds over what I weighed when I got married in 1983, a time in my life when I was in considerably better shape.

After the indulgence of Christmas in 2011, I was literally fed up. I felt sluggish, and the doctor even had me on cholesterol-lowering medication, which was a first for me and freaked me out.

Sleep apnea was a potential concern, and my wife told me how bad my snoring was getting.

In 2012, I would be turning 50 (July 28), and the thought of that created one of those moments in life where you pause, reflect, and resolve to do something different going forward. I even said to myself that I wanted the second half of my life to be different than the first half.

I remembered years back, when my father had lost 30 lbs. and what a difference that made for him. So, I resolved that I would go on a diet starting January 1 and lose 30 lbs. over the next 8 months, by the time I turned 50. It was not a New Year's resolution per se, but I was serious about getting it done.

True to my conviction, I started to diet on January 1–you know, the typical kind that doesn't work so well, makes you feel like you are starving, makes you feel tempted to cheat, is hard to sustain, and where the results only last for short periods afterward. Like millions of others who are constantly trying to lose weight, I just didn't know what else to try.

A few days into January, I was telling a friend about my weight-loss plan. He asked how I was planning to do it and if I had heard of a mobile phone app called MYFitnessPal®. He explained how the app helps you put together a realistic plan, how it provides awareness of the foods you're eating and exercise you're getting, especially the caloric content and burn, and how it helps keep you accountable to a successful result.

That sounded good, so I immediately downloaded MyFitnessPal® and put it to work.

This was my MyFitnessPal® journey:

- I entered my beginning weight…220 lbs. (you need to choose a time of day that you will consistently weigh yourself, so you get an accurate beginning measurement and a comparable daily measure to assess progress).
- I entered my target weight…190 lbs.
- I entered my target completion date…July 28.
- It asked me several questions to determine how active I am on a typical day…I entered moderate (this helps to determine your typical daily caloric burn).
- It provided me with a daily net caloric intake target of 1,770 (this is how many calories I was allowed to consume daily, net of calories burned through exercise, to ensure I would hit my target weight of 190 lbs. by my target completion date of July 28).
- MyFitnessPal® does not tell you what to eat, but it provides you with awareness to make better choices and manage your caloric intake. You literally scan the barcodes on foods with your phone, and MyFitnessPal® tells you the caloric content of a serving (as well as the nutrient content).
- Obviously, exercise is always recommended with most weight loss programs. With MyFitnessPal®, you not only account for calories consumed, but it helps you track the calories burned.
- Every day, I weighed myself and input my weight.
- Every meal, I accounted for what I ate.
- Every time I exercised, I accounted for the calories burned.
- During the day, it showed me how I was tracking, and at the end of every day, it let me know how I did relative to my plan.

So, what happened?

- I was diligent and followed the tracking religiously.
- I exercised a few times a week.
- On average, my net intake was 1,670 calories, which was 100 calories/day less than my target, yet I never starved myself. In fact, starving is a no-no. The key to the whole thing is to change your lifestyle, eat better, and exercise.
- The plan worked so well that I hit my target weight of 190 lbs. in 5 months instead of 8.
- Further, since it was so easy and effective, I continued through to July 28 and ended up losing a total of 50 lbs.

My biggest takeaways:

- MyFitnessPal® provided me with incredible awareness and accountability. Knowing what the caloric content is in foods, like a donut (400-500) or a piece of cheesecake (1,000-2,000+) versus a banana (110), empowered me to make better choices.
- I learned to never starve myself. It's important to keep our metabolism going. So, I carry protein bars with me wherever I go so I never miss or overly delay a meal.
- I follow the king/prince/pauper meal plan: eat a big breakfast like a king (1,000 cal), eat a moderate lunch like a prince (700 cal), and eat almost nothing at dinner like a pauper (300 cal).
- I now maintain a good exercise cadence (about 4x per week).
- I eat healthier – avoid high-calorie meals and try not to eat after 8 pm.

- Practice intentionality by doing little things that are as easy to do as not to do, like taking stairs instead of escalators or elevators whenever possible and realistic.

My passion and affinity for intentionality were ignited through this experience. My understanding and application of intentionality to leadership were developed and refined in the years that followed.

I'm pleased to report that, at the time of publishing this book, a practice of intentionality has enabled me to keep the weight off and maintain a healthier lifestyle for over ten years!

SECTION ONE

FOUNDATIONAL PRINCIPLES AND CONCEPTS

CHAPTER 1

THE DECEPTION OF GOOD INTENTIONS

The road to hell is paved with good intentions.

— SAMUEL L. JOHNSON

The narrow path to heaven is navigated with intentionality.

— HERB K. MAST

In the past, I struggled with Johnson's quote. How could good intentions lead to such a negative result?

Naturally, you'd think that good intentions are a good thing, right? Then why would they lead to hell?

Then, one day, as I started to understand the concept of intentionality, the lightbulb lit up for me. I realized that good intentions are nothing more than just good thoughts. I also realized that good intentions without action and follow-through are meaningless, as they do nothing. I suggest they are worse than nothing, as good intentions without follow-through can do harm. Good intentions typically create expectations and, as pointed out in the backstory, create a void when left unfulfilled.

You see, intentions are like promises. And promises arouse expectations. Promises cause others to adjust their own behaviors and/or get their hopes up that something will happen. And when those promises go unfulfilled, like in Jill's Thanksgiving dinner case, a sense of resentment and cynicism can arise. Hence, it's better not to make a promise and yet do something than to promise and not do it. This explains why it's better to under-promise and over-deliver than the inverse.

There's even a story in the Bible (Matthew 21:28-30) about a father who has two sons. He asks his first son to work in the vineyard. The son says he won't but then feels bad and goes and works in the vineyard. He asks the second son to work in the vineyard. The second son immediately agrees to work in the vineyard, but then doesn't. Jesus asks the crowd around him which of the two sons was the obedient and better son. The crowd responds correctly by saying the first son.

The Bible also warns in an earlier passage, Matthew 5:33-37, against making oaths and then not fulfilling them. A promise is essentially an oath, and Matthew says:

> [33] *Again, you have heard that it was said to the people long ago, 'Do not break your oath, but fulfill to the Lord the vows you have made.'* [34] *But I tell you, do not swear an oath at all: either by heaven, for it is God's throne;* [35] *or by the earth, for it is his footstool; or by Jerusalem, for it is the city of the Great King.* [36] *And do not swear by your head, for you cannot make even one*

> *hair white or black.* [37] *All you need to say is simply 'Yes' or 'No'; anything beyond this comes from the evil one.*[g]

Does that mean we should never make a promise? No, I don't think so. What it suggests is that we need to be careful that we are not flippant with our commitments. Further, we need to be mindful of the consequences of not following through. A better practice is to make a promise only when absolutely necessary and when you are absolutely certain you can and will fulfill it.

So, why do people make promises they are not committed to fulfilling?

Let me use an example to see if it provides insight.

First, think about how we used to write checks in the old days. Nowadays, we almost exclusively use credit or debit cards or some other form of electronic payment, but in the old days, we used to write our promise to pay on rectangular pieces of paper. They were like cash to the person you gave them to—provided there were sufficient funds in the account to cover the amount promised.

Not having enough money in your bank account when the check is presented is a form of fraud and is punishable with fines and/or imprisonment. Writing an NSF (Not Sufficient Funds) check was that serious, although it was rarely treated that way unless the amount was large and/or done in high frequency.

Only con artists and liars make commitments they do not intend to fulfill, right? Well, are we any better when we don't fulfill our commitments, regardless of what those commitments are?

Here's the inherent challenge. We all prefer things now rather than later. We don't like to wait. That is why credit cards have become so popular. They are not only convenient, but we can buy things now, enjoy them now, and delay payment until some point in the future—unlike a check which requires immediate payment once the check is presented to the bank.

Similar to a check, a promise suggests we will do something in the future, rather than now. Each time we purchase something with a credit card, we are making a promise that we will eventually have to fulfill.

Purchasing on credit gets many people into trouble because it's so easy to purchase what we want now and put off the obligation of payment to a future date. The reality is that each credit card purchase creates a debt or obligation, just like every promise creates a debt or obligation.

Provided we fulfill our obligation—pay back the debt when it is due—everything works out fine. Unfortunately, in many cases, since promises are so easy to make without fully considering the consequences, many people make hollow promises and get themselves in trouble.

Credit cards make it easy for many to live beyond their means—acquiring too many things in the moment while accumulating a debt they are unable to repay—resulting in an eventual financial day of reckoning. In 2018, the total U.S. credit card debt exceeded $825 billion (https://www.valuepenguin.com/average-credit-card-debt).

Remember the examples of Jill and Jack above? Creating obligations by making promises too quickly or without due consideration of the consequences can put us in debt to others. And if that debt goes unfulfilled, credibility is compromised, reputation diminished, and relationships altered.

Intentionality is all about being purposeful and deliberate in our actions to optimize positive results and minimize negative ones. This means we are careful with our promises and only make promises we will fulfill.

It is my desire in writing this book that you will not only gain insights into the difference between intentions and intentionality but that you will gain the conviction to live with greater intentionality so that your efforts produce both greater success and fulfillment.

Intentionality is not only a great concept for personal success, but it is a critical practice for leaders and teams. By sheer definition, leadership is about intentional influence in getting a team from one place to another. Leadership and action are directly correlated concepts. It's impossible to be a leader without intentional action.

NOTES AND TAKE-AWAYS

INTENTIONALITY ELEMENTS TO IMPLEMENT

CHAPTER 2

EVEN S.M.A.R.T. GOALS ARE NOT ENOUGH

When it becomes obvious that the goals cannot be achieved, don't adjust the goals, adjust the action steps.

— CONFUCIUS

I had an interesting conversation with a Boy Scout leader one day. I'll call him Mark. I was curious as to the motivation of the leaders of a scout troop. I wondered, why they volunteer their time–what is the reward? I also wondered what the kids, who participated in the program, saw as the benefits–what is the draw?

Mark explained that they come alongside families and invest in boys with the objective of helping them become better citizens of society. The kids have fun, learn lots of skills, and become better people. The volunteers gain the satisfaction, or better stated, fulfillment, of investing in somebody else and making a difference.

Mark also shared with me some of the things he talks to the Scouts about. He mentioned that he explains the value of setting S.M.A.R.T. goals.

S.M.A.R.T. is an acronym for: Specific, Measurable, Achievable, Realistic, and Time-Bound.

After some conversation, I tactfully asked him what part of S.M.A.R.T. goals involve action, or is action implied? After some thought, he admitted that action is implied. This led us into a great conversation about the value and importance of intentionality, which can be enhanced by the five elements of S.M.A.R.T. Without the action part, unfortunately, S.M.A.R.T. goals are no better than good intentions.

I shared with him the Intentionality Model, which I present in a future chapter, and I came away with the sense that he will now include the teaching of intentionality with his Scouts. This is exactly what I hope this book will do—expand the reach of an intentionality message—so many more people will be able to accomplish more of the things they want to achieve because they are focused on purposeful, rather than implied, action.

Talk, goals, and plans are good, but they are not enough. Everybody wants results, and intentionality is that quiet voice that I want to plant in everybody's minds so that, in the process, more things will ultimately get accomplished.

NOTES AND TAKE-AWAYS

INTENTIONALITY ELEMENTS TO IMPLEMENT

CHAPTER 3

PROACTIVITY AND FORWARD LOOKING

I like to encourage people to realize that any action is a good action if it's proactive and there is positive intent behind it.

— MICHAEL J. FOX

People tend to be more reactive than proactive. Research shows that we are hardwired to be reactive in the same way that we are hardwired to protect ourselves from attack, whether that attack is physical or mental.

The problem with reacting is that it doesn't always help us move forward in a positive, purposeful, and consistent manner. Reactive people look at things that already happened, rather than looking forward and figuring out what needs to happen.

Think about annual job reviews. The old standard was that staff were to get a review of their work, behavior, attitude, and a myriad of other elements. Because the annual review was often tied to a raise, many managers would not do the review if they didn't want to give the individual a raise. In the process, not only did the individual lose out on a raise, but they also lost out on valuable feedback relative to the work they did in the past year.

Not only is a year between reviews too long, but by nature of the word, they are backward focused. In a future chapter, I share what I believe to be a much more effective approach, which involves coaching team members to be their best. This involves a more proactive approach by spending more time coaching a person in the things that shape future actions and results.

NOTES AND TAKE-AWAYS

INTENTIONALITY ELEMENTS TO IMPLEMENT

CHAPTER 4

LAGGING VERSUS LEADING INDICATORS

Ultimately, what any company does when it is successful is merely a lagging indicator of its existing culture.

— SATYA NADELLA

Lagging indicators are metrics that focus on what has already happened, while a leading indicator focuses on the actions that will produce the results that will eventually become a lagging indicator.

Financial statements are lagging indicators. The number of sales calls a salesperson makes is the leading indicator.

Your bathroom scale is a lagging indicator. The food you eat and the exercise you undertake are leading indicators.

The wake of a boat is a lagging indicator. The turns you make with a boat steering wheel are leading indicators.

Lagging indicators are only helpful in as much as they validate whether the actions taken produced the desired result. Hence, we need both lagging and leading indicators to produce results in line with our goals and objectives.

There is a funny statement that talks about somebody driving fast in the wrong direction and making good time but not knowing where they're going.

You can get in your car and start driving, but we typically don't get in our cars without clarity of the destination. Maps are a great tool to help us get pointed in the right direction and to know what turns to take to get to our destination. Maps are good, but interactive GPS systems are better—a system that not only details the route we should take but tells us when we're off track. An interactive GPS system is an example of an intentionality tool.

I suggest that leaders adopt the 80/20 rule when it comes to lagging and leading indicators—focus 80% of your time and efforts on leading actions and only 20% on lagging indicators. Unfortunately, too many managers get this flipped and spend 80% looking backward. It's not surprising then why they don't produce results as good as they could.

NOTES AND TAKE-AWAYS

INTENTIONALITY ELEMENTS TO IMPLEMENT

CHAPTER 5

NEUROSCIENCE AND LEADERSHIP

Everything we do, every thought we've ever had, is produced by the human brain. But exactly how it operates remains one of the biggest unsolved mysteries, and it seems the more we probe its secrets, the more surprises we find.

— NEIL DEGRASSE TYSON

It would be difficult, if not impossible, to write a book entitled *Intentionality for Leaders* without digging into a little neuroscience, especially since I define leadership as intentional influence.

Understanding how the brain works is helpful for both intentionality and influence. Further, if you want to influence somebody intentionally, it's important to understand how human beings are wired and what things influence people more than other things.

The study of the brain (neuroscience) reveals that our emotional brain (Limbic) drives three times more behaviors than our rational brain (Neocortex).

The rational brain is responsible for logical and analytical thinking, whereas the emotional brain is responsible for processing feelings. The reason this is important for leaders to know is because 75% of what we do is due to the influence of the emotional brain and only 25% because of the logic behind our thoughts. In other words, we are three times more likely to do something because we feel like doing it, regardless of the rational data available to us. The reason we often believe our rational brains are more influential is because of the rational brain's ability to rationalize why we did something.

Ask any child why they did something that didn't seem to make sense, and they will usually say, "Because I felt like it."

Another important piece of neuroscience is that our ability to speak comes from the rational brain. The emotional brain has no ability to speak—but feels and interprets the surroundings, body language, tone, choice of words, etc. to develop a gut feeling. For example, if I were to ask you what you had for dinner last night, you could easily tell me in detail. But, if I were to ask how you felt about dinner last night, you might have to pause to process your feelings and help your rational brain choose appropriate words. Your answer would vary between the two extremes of "hated it" and "loved it," with almost endless possibilities in between.

Since feelings drive three times more behavior, it's important to understand whether something is rational or emotional and focus on the emotional elements to drive more behavior.

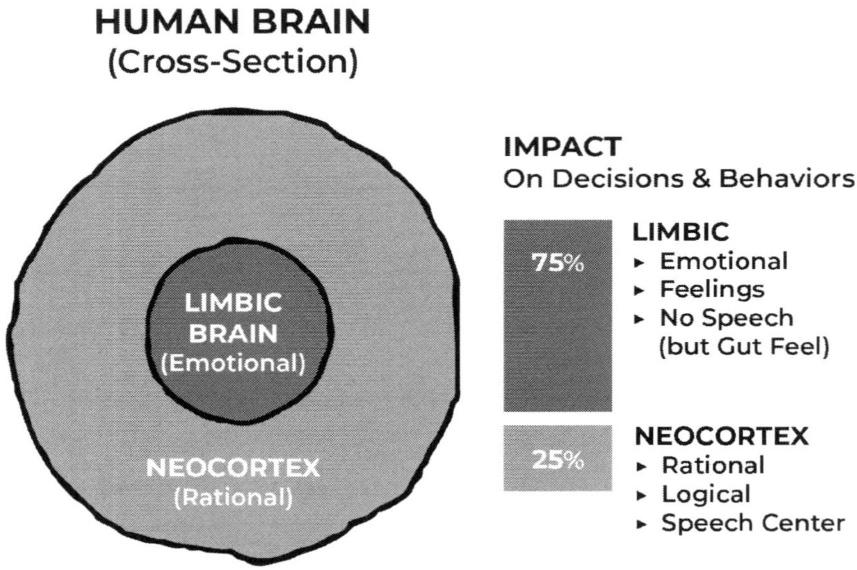

A good way to know whether something is rational is to ask yourself whether it can be measured. Rational things are black and white and can be measured. Emotional things are grey-scale and hard to quantify.

Computers operate in the rational realm and process data in strings of ones and zeros (e.g. 111001011000) called binary language. Computers are great at processing lots of data and assisting in decision making, based on clear rules built into the code of the program. Computers, however, cannot process feelings. Processing feelings requires a Limbic brain.

Knowing that feelings drive three times more behavior is important to a leader because, as an intentional influencer, a leader wants to drive as much behavior as possible to effect better results. So, it's important to be able to determine whether something is rational or emotional.

If something can be measured or answered in a yes or no manner, it's typically rational. To be able to determine if something is emotional, you need to ask a different kind of question, a question where yes or no doesn't fit and where the answer is more grayscale. I prefer using a scale of 1-10 or 0-10. There's nothing special about 1-10. It could be 1-5 or 1-100. It could also be any multiple-choice approach, like: strongly disagree, somewhat disagree, neither agree nor disagree, somewhat agree, or strongly agree. This is essentially a scale of -2, -1, 0, +1, +2.

The point is, for emotional questions, you want to give the emotional brain options so it can better decide how it feels and what answer best fits that feeling.

When defining the upper and lower limits of scaled options, it is helpful to make the upper and lower limits extreme. For example, the lower limit can be defined as "hate" and the upper limit "love."

Let's consider a few examples. First, let's assume I want to know what your favorite dessert is. I could ask whether you like ice cream. This begs the answer of either yes or no, which is not helpful as a person could answer yes but not really like ice cream very much.

So, I would get a more insightful answer by asking, "Using a scale of 0 to 10, where 0 represents hating it and 10 represents the best dessert ever, how much do you like ice cream?" I've asked this question many times in groups to prove a point, and it's fascinating how most people who would answer "yes" that they like ice cream can answer as low as 2 in a 0-10 question.

Since I'm trying to determine what somebody's favorite dessert is, I could ask a follow-up question, "What would be a 10 for you?" The answer I often hear is, "chocolate," which would also be my response.

This is helpful when I want to do something special for somebody and need to know how somebody feels. If I know that a person only likes ice cream at the 6/10 level, but likes chocolate at the 9/10 level, it would be better to get them a chocolate cake for their birthday than an ice cream cake.

This simple insight is powerful not only to make people feel better, but to influence their behavior or to determine their level of passion for something.

Imagine that I'm a head football coach looking to hire assistant coaches and recruit players. One of the most helpful questions right off the top is to ask them to rate how much they love the game of football, using a scale of 1-10 where 1 is "I don't care for the game" and 10 is "it's the best game ever!" What number would I want, even need, to hear for a person to qualify for further consideration?

Whenever I ask this question in group settings, everybody responds with "10" or even "11."

When hiring somebody, rather than asking a prospective new hire whether they have experience or skill in certain areas, it's more helpful to know, on a scale of 1-10, where 1 represents little to no skill and 10 represents being a master, how would they rate their level of skill? The number they choose tells us a lot and opens the door for further conversation to gain even greater insights into their potential fit with the job and the organization.

For another example, I'm going to lean on my experience coaching for Ford Motor Company. In 2015, Ford introduced a "love" question in their consumer surveys. The Ford Dealers hated it and, while it was hard to explain, it gave me a platform to explain how the brain and intentional influence work.

The question was worded like this:

> *Please rate how you feel about the following statement, "I love XYZ Ford"* (where XYZ was the actual name of the dealer that either sold or serviced the vehicle).
>
> Strongly disagree...somewhat disagree...neither agree nor disagree...somewhat agree...strongly agree

Unfortunately, though this question was excellent in gaining insights into how customers felt about the dealership (86% of customers actually answered that they strongly agree), too many dealers hated the question because they didn't understand it and seemed to persuade Ford to remove it (which they did after a few years).

Yes, love is a strong sentiment, the most positive sentiment, in fact. That's the point. Ford and their consultants wanted to measure how likely that customer was to become a repeat customer and how likely they were to refer somebody to the dealership. And, since feelings drive behaviors three times more than rational factors, it was a great question, and predictor of loyalty.

Since feelings can be messy, many managers steer clear to more familiar territory that they can also better control...like, money. But money is rational and only influences 25% of behaviors. If money were truly the great panacea that trumps everything else, nobody would quit a higher paying job to take a lower paying job with a better environment, nobody would take a vacation, nobody would eat out, no parent would choose to stay home with their children, nobody would volunteer their time to further the cause of a non-profit organization, etc.

Sure, we all need a certain amount of money to survive, but ultimately, money, being rational, can be trumped by something that makes us feel better. That's why I stand by the statement that "it's never about the money!" I frequently welcome groups that I coach to challenge me on this, and it always makes for spirited debate, until I point out that money is just a medium of exchange. We trade money for things we would rather have, like time, happiness, health, fun, convenience, food, shelter, education, vacations, etc. In the end it's almost always for things that are influenced by our feelings.

Leaders who get this look past the money aspect and ask better questions of their people to determine what things they like and then help the person achieve more of those things.

Learning to ask better questions helps leaders do a better job of connecting with and influencing others. To this end, the art of asking 1-10 scale questions is powerful and will be applied much throughout the rest of this book.

So, to be more intentional and a greater influencer, you need to understand how the brain works and then work with the natural way the brain works to match people with more things they want to do than just things people do because they are being paid to do them.

Later in the book, I will touch on the concept of gutfeel, which is also rooted in our emotional brain. Gutfeel is another powerful tool for leaders, as often they don't have all the empirical evidence, they would like in order to make a decision. But because of how the emotional brain works in gathering and processing unspoken information, learning to trust your gut is very helpful.

This is especially true when it comes to building and maintaining trust, which most don't realize is a combination of both rational and emotional factors.

TRUST

RATIONAL 25%	EMOTIONAL 75%
▸ Competence	▸ Authenticity
▸ Reliability	▸ Care

Most people rely on building trust in a rational manner and then are surprised that a small slip-up with one of the emotional elements results in them losing trust with somebody.

The car business provides lots of great examples of how this works. Imagine a car salesman that knows their product inside and out (competence) and follows through with the things they say during the transaction (reliability) but doesn't respond quickly, if at all, to your calls after the sale (lack of care) and sends you an automated email of thanks (lack of authenticity).

Many car salespeople are great talkers before the sale but use the same language as every other car salesperson out there. Then they wonder why people don't trust them.

If this were not true, Used Car Salesmen would not have gained the reputation they have over the years.

NOTES AND TAKE-AWAYS

INTENTIONALITY ELEMENTS TO IMPLEMENT

CHAPTER 6

THE ESSENCE OF LEADERSHIP

Leaders do not force others to follow,
they invite them on a journey.

— CHARLES S. LAUER

Few of us can journey alone for long. In fact, humans are hard-wired for connection. In other words, we need each other if we are to develop and perform at our best.

Well known author and clinical psychologist, Henry Cloud, in his book, *The Power of the Other*, shares that our brains need three things to survive: oxygen, glucose (food), and connection [with other human beings].

We all have a need to be connected and share experiences with others. That is why solitary confinement is considered a brutal form of punishment. There are also many studies that have been done with infants to assess the impact of nurturing on the development of the child. Interestingly, it has been discovered that the brains of orphans who do not get the same level of nurturing as other children do not develop as well.

Connection is critical to the health and well-being of humans and other species.

And whenever there is a group of people who want to accomplish something, not only is it critical that a leader emerge from within the ranks, but invariably, somebody does emerge to provide the group with direction and inspiration to accomplish the objective.

This book is not intended to replace other leadership books. There are thousands, if not millions, of books that have already been published on the topic of leadership. Rather, this is a book focused on raising awareness for the concept of intentionality that has tremendous application in the realm of leadership. This book provides leaders, and others, with a better understanding of what intentionality is and how it can be applied to achieve better results for individuals, teams, and leaders. That being said, I believe it's helpful to provide foundational insights into what a leader is, especially from an intentionality perspective, before diving into specific intentionality-based tools for leaders.

In its simplest form, the role of a leader is to get a team from here to there. It's that simple!

In other words, the core objective of leaders is to get a team from wherever they are now [HERE] to somewhere else [THERE].

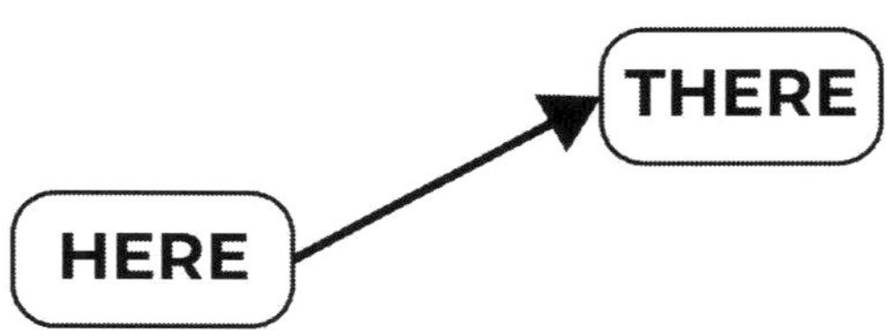

We don't need leaders if we simply want to stay where we are now. We may need managers and bosses but not leaders.

Leaders are intentional influencers. Not manipulators, coercers, tyrants, nor dictators.

Leaders intentionally influence people to take specific, coordinated, and intentional actions that allow a team to get where that team collectively wants to go effectively and efficiently. Teams that are led by a true leader tend to have a sense of purpose in the things they do.

Many people falsely believe leaders, managers, and bosses are synonymous concepts. This is one of the most dangerous delusions, especially for people in positions of power.

Before focusing on leadership in the next few paragraphs, let me make two brief, and sufficient, statements about management and bosses.

Nobody likes to be managed. The best way to look at it is that you manage things, and you lead people. Management is often associated with an approach called "command and control," whereas leadership uses an approach of "trust and inspire."

The word boss seems to be self-explanatory. A boss bosses or tells others what to do, whether they want to do it or not. Nobody wants to be bossed. Bossing only feels good when you're on the giving end, although even then, the act of bossing takes a lot of energy and provides little fulfillment.

Leadership, on the other hand, is all about others and the common things the group or team wants to accomplish.

Unfortunately, there are many people in positions of power who are not leaders and rather are managers or bosses. There are also many people who are leaders who don't have the traditional title to go along with it. Leadership does not require a title, and a title does not make somebody a leader.

Leadership is about intentional influence. That is why good communication and good leadership tend to go hand in hand.

As Charles Lauer, mentor to generations of healthcare workers across the United States, so astutely observed, *true leaders don't force people to follow; they invite them on a journey*.

It's important to understand that leadership is a choice and a skill that can be developed by virtually anybody. People are not born leaders. They choose whether they are willing to humble themselves to the cause and the team and whether they will accept the responsibilities associated with leadership.

I happen to believe that anyone can be a leader if they so choose and embrace the responsibilities associated with leading, but not everyone should be a leader.

As stated above, the essence of leadership is getting people from one place to another. And the reality is that some people are more suited to leading. Whether it's a personality thing or just confidence, some people seem to recognize, even desire, leadership opportunities—taking on greater responsibility and directing others. For others, it can be a calling. Some would say it even comes more naturally for some people. While I agree that some personalities may be better suited to leading, I don't believe that people are born leaders.

In his book, *The Motive*, Patrick Lencioni challenges would-be leaders to search their motive for leading. He suggests there are two types of leaders, rewards-based leaders and responsibility (or results)-based leaders.

A rewards-based leader is a person who is more motivated by what's in it for them. Many people have selfish motivations and use their platform or position to gain greater power, authority, position, money, etc.—i.e., rewards. These people are like mercenaries, guns for hire, who pursue leadership opportunities for what they will gain in the process.

A responsibility (or results)-based leader is a person who does things for the benefit of others. Sure, they enjoy the rewards, but their motivation is the greater good of the team and society. They see rewards as the byproduct. These people are what we might refer to as patriots—they put love of country first and rewards second.

Lencioni suggests that a leader's attitude and embrace of five key responsibilities demonstrates what kind of leader they are. A rewards-based leader tends to abdicate the following responsibilities:

1. Having difficult and uncomfortable conversations with others.
2. Managing direct-reports.
3. Running great meetings.
4. Developing a cohesive team.
5. Being the chief reminding officer.

In abdicating these responsibilities, a leader avoids providing the direction team members need to do and become their best and, in the process, produce great results.

Some might question why anybody would choose responsibilities over rewards. We all understand how rewards can be motivating, even addictive, but might wonder how responsibility could provide adequate motivation—since the reward is not the focus. I hope the following story will provide insights.

Imagine you are doing your weekly grocery shopping. After amassing a cart full of food and sundries, you proceed to the cashier. One other party is in front of you. It appears to be a mother with two young children. One is only a few months old and is sleeping in a car seat. The other is a toddler, who is sitting in the cart and playing with some of the items. The young mother is placing her items on the belt—milk, cheese, eggs, vegetables, fruit, diapers, etc. the basics.

The total comes to about forty dollars, and the mother proceeds to pay with a credit card. To both her and your surprise, her card is declined. She turns red, and after a brief pause of embarrassment, she proceeds to put the items back in her cart.

You see the whole thing unfold. An opportunity has presented itself. What do you do?

Mercenaries could argue they bear no responsibility and would let the mother fend for herself.

Patriots, on the other hand, see an opportunity to do something for the greater good. They feel compelled to act and readily provide their own credit card, or cash, to pay for this young family's groceries. There are no reporters capturing the moment on film, and you won't be on the evening news, something that might motivate a mercenary, but you do the good deed regardless. In the process, you do get a reward. One from within…a blessing…a good feeling…a feeling of satisfaction that money can't buy.

Earlier in the book, I shared that feelings are a powerful motivational force. In fact, research reveals that feelings motivate three times more actions and behaviors than rational elements alone. As detailed above, it comes from how our brain is wired.

The foregoing story provides an example of the internal motivation that drives responsibility-based leaders. A motivation that can be three times more powerful than typical rewards, like money.

The takeaway is that leadership is a choice, moment by moment. In this way, leaders are developed and shaped by their choices over time. This is good news, as without leaders, our journey would take longer and with far fewer results.

When speaking to groups of businesspeople about leadership, I often start a new session by asking the group how many volunteers they have in their organization. Most have the deer-in-the-headlights stare as they ponder my question. The answer usually comes back as, "None." I then ask a follow-up question, "How many volunteers should we have in our organization?" Again, I get the deer-in-the-headlights stare and a long pause as most people don't know what to say. I intentionally let them ponder the question before I share with them about the difference between power and authority.

In a power-based environment, people do things because they have to, while in an authority-based environment, people do things because they choose to or want to.

In a power-based organization, also referred to as a command-and-control environment, we are essentially renting the hands and feet of people. Another way of looking at this is from a motivation standpoint. Power tends to infer that motivation comes from extrinsic, or external, factors—the proverbial carrots and sticks. Examples of carrots are: titles, money, bonuses, incentives, rewards, fame, etc. Sticks refer to punishments, penalties, and disincentives.

In an authority-based organization, also referred to as a trust and inspire environment, people are willing to volunteer their hearts and minds. In this kind of environment, people are more motivated by intrinsic, or internal, factors.

In his book, *Drive—The Surprising Truth About What Motivates Us*, Daniel Pink reveals that the three main intrinsic motivators are autonomy, mastery, and purpose.

Autonomy: The freedom to choose my own path and be self-directed.

In my line of work, I travel extensively. I schedule dates and times with my clients and then figure out the details of how I'm going to get there, where I'm going to stay, and which other clients I'm going to visit on the same trip. I choose how I'm going to execute the scope of work. Nobody tells me where I'm going to go and when. I'm convinced that, by having such autonomy, I'm not only able to handle a much larger workload but am more committed to keeping my schedule even when flights get canceled or delayed and find the work much more fulfilling than if somebody told me where I would travel each week.

Mastery: Becoming the best I can be at my craft or chosen activity.

None of us is good at everything, but each of us has an affinity and knack for something. The key is matching the needed activity with the desired activity of the individual. I have a passion for golf and invest a tremendous amount of time and money practicing, watching, and playing golf, even though I don't get paid to do so. I could say the same for my study of leadership, culture, and teamwork, which is something I do get paid for. But I don't have an affinity or knack for playing the piano. I love listening to a good pianist, and I even tried to learn in my youth but just never developed an affinity for it. Therefore, I'm not motivated to work at it, even if somebody were to pay me to do it.

Purpose: Fighting for a cause.

We all care about something, if not many things. And the more we care, the more effort we are willing to put into protecting or furthering that something, whether it be an idea, vision, need, philosophy, or belief. The essence of business is defined as, "Find a need and fill it." Patriots are fueled by love of country and are willing to sacrifice everything, including their lives, to ensure their country is protected.

Purpose is a powerful motivator and needs to be one of the biggest reasons we work for an organization. Simon Sinek, in his book *Start with Why*, presents the case for organizations hiring people who identify and align with Why the organization exists. People will accept lower pay just to work for an organization whose vision and mission they believe in. This has much to do with the emotional brain and how it drives three times more behavior than the rational brain. You don't need to look further than non-profit organizations where people will even volunteer their time (i.e., for no pay) to help further a cause.

Patrick Lencioni, in his book *The Advantage—Why Organizational Health Trumps Everything Else in Business*, suggests that the first question the leadership of every organization must answer is: *Why do we exist?* In other words, what is the organization there to accomplish? The answer cannot simply be to make money. The why of the organization must connect with people at their core for it to be transformative. This is why it's so important for an organization to put serious effort into formulating a meaningful vision and mission statement that their people can align with and rally around. Unfortunately, too many organizations see this as a box to check rather than a mantra that will help to motivate and guide their team every step of the journey.

Here is a great graphic I came across in the 1990s that I tweaked over the years to capture the essence of team member engagement.

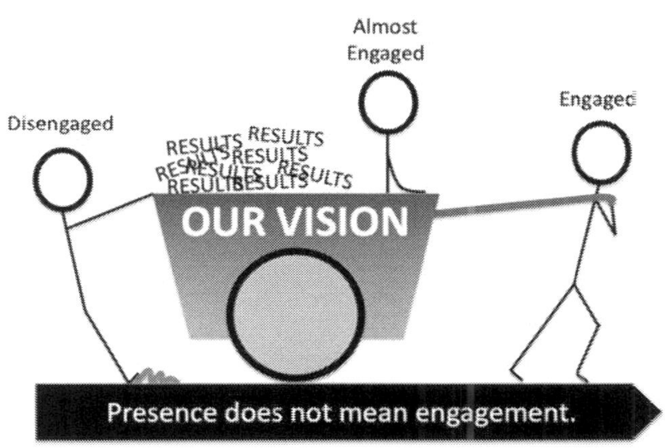

Engaged team members are the ones out front, putting in the greatest effort to pull the cart (vision, mission, and values of the organization) forward. Results, usually measured by money in for-profit organizations, are not the goal but the by-product of living the vision, executing the mission, and providing fuel for the journey.

The more you study neuroscience, the more you learn that our emotional [Limbic] brains, the intrinsic center, drive three times more behavior than our rational [Neocortex] brains. This is relevant when you intentionally want to influence people's behaviors, which is the essence of leadership.

The biological fact is that, under stress and pressure, our bodies produce a hormone called cortisol that intentionally shuts down our emotional brains and puts us into a reactive state. This is part of our survival system so that we can better react to threats, like when we are fending off an attacker. In these types of situations, it's more important to act fast to preserve our safety than ponder what we might feel like for lunch. The cortisol stops us from thinking about our feelings and just gets us to act, which is great when trying to survive but not so great when needing to work better as a team.

So, in low-stress and positive environments, our emotional brain is able to function well and is able to contribute more of our best work—creativity, innovation, collaboration, and building relationships. Unfortunately, the exercise of power by managers and bosses imposes pressure and stress, which has the effect of shutting down the emotional brain and activating the rational brain.

In his book, *The Servant*, James Hunter does a great job of comparing and contrasting power and authority and helping would-be leaders understand the difference. He paraphrases the definitions offered by Max Weber, one of the founders of the field of sociology, as follows:

Power: The ability to force or coerce someone to do your will, even if they would choose not to, because of your position or might.

Authority: The skill of getting people to willingly do your will because of your personal influence.

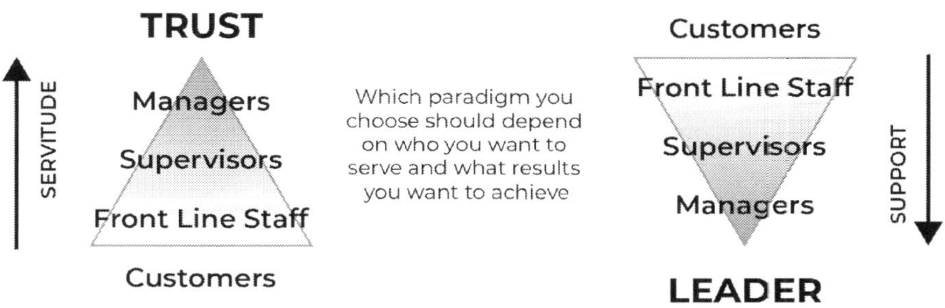

(Hunter: The Servant)

Politicians exercise power in enacting laws. Policemen enforce power by giving out tickets or making arrests when people choose to defy those laws. This is the act of forcing people to follow—something generally done more by bosses and managers.

In contrast, leaders invite people on a journey. Leaders intentionally influence people to buy into the vision, mission, and values of the organization. They seek out people who align with what the organization is attempting to do and why it's being done.

Pastors would be a great example of somebody who exercises authority, providing insights into a better way and inviting people to follow.

An interesting dichotomy is how true leaders rarely need to exert power to effect change and get others to follow, while posing leaders are ineffective without title or position to impose their wills on others. Posers tend to use fear, power, and intimidation to get others to do things, while real leaders inspire others and focus on shared purpose to elicit effort and effect change.

The difference between influence and manipulation is said to be intent. The more I study the art and science of leadership, the more amazed I am that would-be leaders don't get it. Why would you use a formula that produces one-third of the results compared to another formula? If using influence and exerting authority drives three times more behaviors, why would anybody resort to manipulation and exerting power to get things done? I'm convinced it comes down to two reasons: lack of awareness—don't know that there is a better way because nobody has told them, or lack of humility—don't care that there is a better way because it doesn't feed their ego and need for control.

A great reminder is that you manage things and lead people.

Our businesses, governments, churches, and organizations, and the people both dependent on and/or serving in them, would be better served if those at the top of the organizational chart did some soul-searching to determine if they truly want to lead, follow, or need to get out of the way.

Too many lives have and are being detrimentally impacted by people who are posing as leaders but who don't have the passion, capability, or capacity to lead. All too often, these posers exert power and coercion to get people to do things.

Much of this book is devoted to helping shape you into a great leader by providing insights into the many important actions that define great leaders and inspiring you to incorporate those actions into your playbook and to lead with intentionality.

First, however, a challenge to those who want to be leaders: If you choose to be a leader—Lead! Otherwise, be a good follower. Either way, don't impede the progress of the team!

NOTES AND TAKE-AWAYS

INTENTIONALITY ELEMENTS TO IMPLEMENT

CHAPTER 7

LEAD, FOLLOW, OR GET OUT OF THE WAY

Lead, follow, or get out of the way.

— THOMAS PAINE

Some are leaders. Others are followers. Neither is better than the other. We need both cooperating with each other to achieve things. The key is being authentic to who you are and the talents and abilities you have been given.

Thomas Paine, who authored two influential pamphlets at the start of the American Revolution and inspired the patriots in 1776 to declare independence from Great Britain, said, "Lead, follow, or get out of the way!"

Regardless of whether you are a leader or a follower, we are all on a journey. In fact, the human condition requires every person to journey—we are hardwired to pursue a cause. To survive, let alone thrive, everybody needs to feel they are making a difference. It is a huge part of what motivates us to get up each day.

This book is not so much about helping you to find your purpose as it is about helping you consistently to take action that is aligned with your sense of purpose and philosophy for life and business. Although, if in the process of better understanding intentionality and leadership, you are able to connect more dots of purpose in your journey, that would be a bonus.

This is also not intended to be a book that helps you figure out whether you are a good leader or a better follower, although many of the topics addressed herein may cause you to wrestle with why you do what you do.

This book is intended to provide general awareness and simple practical actions that both leaders and followers can adopt to achieve greater results in the 24 hours each of us is given each day.

NOTES AND TAKE-AWAYS

INTENTIONALITY ELEMENTS TO IMPLEMENT

CHAPTER 8

EVERYBODY HAS AT LEAST A PENNY

True wealth is not of the pocket, but of the heart and of the mind.

— KEVIN GATES

Many people never get started on their journey to "success" because they either don't feel they have anything to start with, they fear failure, or they simply feel inadequate. Instead, they give up before they even get started.

Fear has paralyzed many people and kept many great ideas from seeing the light of day. Fear and inadequacy seem to be closely related naysayers.

Another reason many people never get started is that they do not feel they have anything to contribute.

The good news is that all of us have something to contribute to society, even if it is just a penny.

What good is a penny, you might ask?

The exciting thing about intentionality is that you need very little to get started. Even a penny will do. Let me demonstrate with a story.

A father was diagnosed with advanced pancreatic cancer and given less than 30 days to live. Realizing he did not have much time left to spend with his family, he tried to make the best of every moment and ensure his affairs were in order.

One day, the father sat with his twin college-age children and shared from his heart.

First, he wanted them to know their mother would be well taken care of. He told them how his business efforts had been blessed, and over the years, he had accumulated a fair amount of wealth. He wanted them to know that it did not come without hard work, but it was more the result of making good decisions along the way.

Second, he wanted to give them a choice that he hoped would help them make better decisions and take intentional positive actions in their lives.

He opened his left hand to reveal a check for a million dollars. Then he opened his right hand to reveal a penny. He told them that they could choose either the million dollars or the penny.

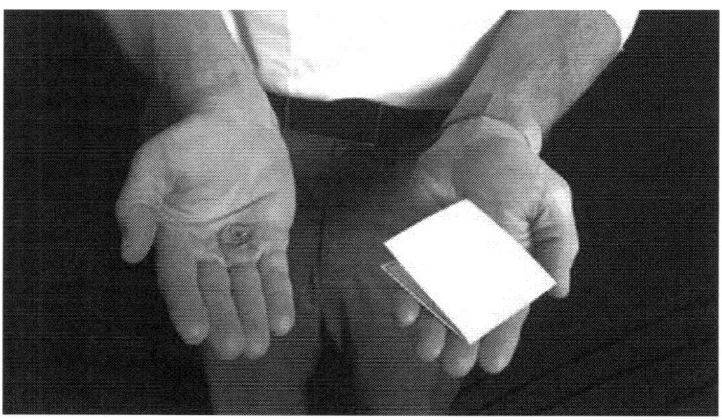

He asked them to ponder their decision for 24 hours. In the meantime, he asked them to consider all the factors and make the best decision possible. He explained that, regardless of which of the two options they chose, they could not have the money immediately but would need to wait 30 days.

He took out a red velvet drawstring bag and put the million-dollar check in it. Then he took out a black velvet drawstring bag and put the penny in it.

He explained that, during the next 30 days, if they chose the million dollars, they could go to the bank and borrow against the million dollars and spend, invest, or do anything else they wanted with the loans. At the end of the 30 days, their mother would pay off the bank loan and give them the balance.

If they chose the penny, each day over the next 30 days, their mother would double the amount of money in the black drawstring bag. He explained that, on the first day, their mother would add another penny so there would be two. On the second day, she would add two more so there would be four. On the third day, she would add four more so there would be eight. And so on.

He also handed them each a copy of a little book entitled *The Compound Effect* and suggested that it would help them make their choice.

Without knowing anything further, consider right now which of the two options you would choose—the million dollars or the penny.

Both children were distraught that their father was dying and tried to take in what he was telling them.

As the children went to their rooms to consider their options, the first child could not help but think of all the things he could spend the money on. His mind was going a mile a minute, and he had a hard time sleeping.

The second child also had a hard time sleeping, wondering why their father would give them such a choice and why one of the options was a penny. Clearly, the million dollars was tempting, but she also knew her father to be a wise man who always had good reasoning behind the things he did. As she lay in bed pondering her options, she grabbed the little book her father had given them and started to read.

In the morning, the first child came and announced that he would take the million dollars. Shortly thereafter, the second child stated that she would take the penny. The first child looked at her in disbelief and even mocked her a little.

The next few days became a blur as their father's health deteriorated quickly. Within days, he passed away.

It wasn't until the tenth day that the children had time to think about their choices. The first child was curious how much the penny had amounted to. Their mother opened the black drawstring bag to reveal that the penny had increased to $10.24. The first child had a hard time holding back a smug grin, knowing that he had chosen the million.

The children agreed to get back together on the twentieth day, at which time they found the penny had increased to $10,485.76. Again, the first child ribbed his sister and told her how he had gotten a loan like their father said he could and how he had already purchased a new car and several other expensive toys that he had always wanted.

Over the next week, the first child continued to spend and party with his friends while the second child patiently waited for the thirtieth day to come.

On the thirtieth day, the first child received $490,000 dollars after the bank loans were paid off. The first child, still felt a little smug, thinking he had made the better choice until their mother opened the black drawstring bag and pulled out a note. She told them that the bag couldn't contain all the pennies, so she kept track of the accumulating value on a piece of paper. She passed the note to the second child, who unfolded it to reveal the amount of $10,737,418.24.

The first child's jaw dropped. He questioned how this could be possible. Their mother assured him the math was correct (see Appendix B for the calculations) and proceeded to share with him the principle of intentionality as detailed in the little book their father had given them. The first child admitted that he had not taken the time to read the book. He said that the decision seemed like a no-brainer, and rather, he turned his attention towards what he could do with his windfall.

His mother tried to help him understand that, while he had not made the better of the two decisions, he could still turn the remaining money into great value if he put the Intentionality Model to work.

Intentionality is not about what we start with but what we do with what we have. And the good news is we all have at least a penny to start with.

As a reminder of the power of a penny, I started putting a penny in my pocket each morning. This habit reminded me each morning, and each time I put my hands in my pocket, to do the little things that are as easy to do as they are not to do. This simple reminder helps me to seize many opportunities throughout the day that I would otherwise have ignored.

I have created an intentionality penny. It serves as a tool to share my story with others, in hopes they will be inspired to accomplish something they have been putting off. The penny also has an intentional hole in the middle as a reminder of the interplay between the two important parts of the brain—rational and emotional—more on this further in the book.

(Shown here at twice the actual size)

Scan this QR code if you would like to get one or more intentionality pennies.

NOTES AND TAKE-AWAYS

INTENTIONALITY ELEMENTS TO IMPLEMENT

CHAPTER 9

THE RIDER, THE ELEPHANT, AND THE PATH

Wanting something is not enough. You must hunger for it. Your motivation must be absolutely compelling in order to overcome the obstacles that will invariably come your way.

— LES BROWN

Humans are emotional beings, but few understand how powerful our emotions are when it comes to motivation and follow-through. As previously stated, understanding how our brains work is central to embracing the benefits of intentionality, especially as it relates to leadership.

There is a great analogy that helps us understand the interplay and tension between the two parts of our brains and understand how to tap into the appropriate parts of our brain to get more done.

The analogy used by University of Virginia psychologist Jonathan Haidt in his book *The Happiness Hypothesis* involves an Elephant, a Rider, and a Path.

The size and weight of an average elephant is 9-10 feet tall and 9,000 pounds. The size and weight of the average man is about 5 feet 10 inches tall and 180 pounds.

Imagine a man riding an elephant down a clear, smooth path. The Elephant weighs fifty times more than the Rider. The Rider has a plan and thinks he is the leader. By all intents and purposes, as long as the Elephant and the Rider agree on which direction to go, the Rider is able to make progress toward his plan—assuming no insurmountable obstacles are encountered on the path. However, whenever the Elephant and Rider disagree, the Rider is going to lose, like when the hungry Elephant spots a luscious banana grove. Suddenly, a new plan takes over.

The Elephant changes direction, and all the Rider can do is hang on. The original plan no longer matters. The Path remains a factor, but generally, the Elephant will do whatever it wants.

In this analogy, the Elephant is a metaphor for our emotional brain, the Rider is a metaphor for our rational brain, and the Path is a metaphor for our environment or situation.

We come up with plans with our rational brain, plans that make sense and will accomplish certain objectives. Then, and for various reasons, our emotional brain often hijacks our plan and takes us on a ride somewhere else.

ONE BRAIN, TWO MINDS

- **ELEPHANT = IMPULSIVE MIND**
- **RIDER = RATIONAL MIND**
- **PATH = THE ENVIRONMENT**

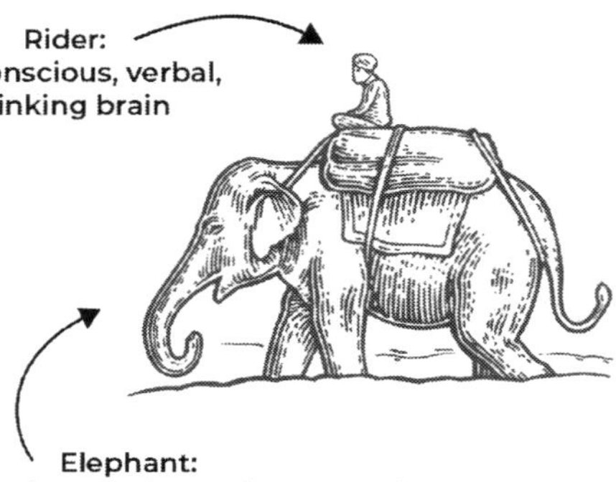

WILLPOWER IS THE STRENGTH OF THE RIDER

(Haidt, 2006)

Dan and Chip Heath, in their book *Switch—How to Change Things When Change is Hard*, refer to this analogy and suggest the weakness of the Elephant, our emotional and instinctive side, is clear: It's lazy and skittish, often looking for the quick payoff (ice cream) over the long-term payoff (being thin). When change efforts fail, it's usually the Elephant's fault, since the kinds of change we typically want involve short-term sacrifices for long-term payoffs.

The Heaths claim that changes often fail because the Rider simply can't keep the Elephant on the road long enough to reach the destination.

On the next page are tips on how to effect change.

I'd like to offer a personal example to provide insights into how simply and pervasively our brain impacts our daily activities. In the beginning of this book, I shared my story of losing 50 pounds over an eight-month period just before I turned 50. Over the next number of years, I have been able to maintain my lower and desired weight by practicing intentionality. This has involved both my eating habits and exercise routines.

I'm going to share the store in terms of my Rider, Elephant, and the Path to bring the analogy to life.

Mornings tend to be the best time for me to exercise. It seems to be when I can block time in my schedule, but it also happens to be the time I feel like it the least. To maintain a regular exercise routine, you need to find a time that works for you and when you feel like it the most. Be careful, however, not to let your Elephant convince you to procrastinate until a later part of the day, just to find yourself out of time or too tired.

HOW TO MAKE A SWITCH

For things to change, somebody somewhere has to start acting differently. Maybe it's you, maybe it's your team. Picture that person (or people).

Each has an emotional Elephant side and a rational Rider side. You've got to reach both. And you've also got to clear the way for them to succeed. In short, you must do three things:

DIRECT the Rider

FOLLOW THE BRIGHT SPOTS. Investigate what's working and clone it. [Jerry Sternin in Vietnam, solutions-focused therapy]

SCRIPT THE CRITICAL MOVES. Don't think big picture, think in terms of specific behaviors. [1% milk, four rules at the Brazilian railroad]

POINT TO THE DESTINATION. Change is easier when you know where you're going and why it's worth it. ["You'll be third graders soon," "No dry holes" at BP]

MOTIVATE the Elephant

FIND THE FEELING. Knowing something isn't enough to cause change. Make people feel something. [Piling gloves on the table, the chemotherapy video game, Robyn Waters's demons at Target]

SHRINK THE CHANGE. Break down the change until it no longer spooks the Elephant. [The 5-Minute Room Rescue, procurement reform]

GROW YOUR PEOPLE. Cultivate a sense of identity and instill the growth mindset. [Brasilata's "inventors," junior-high math kids' turnaround]

SHAPE the Path

TWEAK THE ENVIRONMENT. When the situation changes, the behavior changes. So change the situation. [Throwing out the phone system at Rackspace, 1-Click ordering, simplifying the online time sheet]

BUILD HABITS. When behavior is habitual, it's "free"—it doesn't tax the Rider. Look for ways to encourage habits. [Setting "action triggers," eating two bowls of soup while dieting, using checklists]

RALLY THE HERD. Behavior is contagious. Help it spread. ["Fataki" in Tanzania, "free spaces" in hospitals, seeding the tip jar]

To maintain a regular exercise routine, my Rider typically chooses mornings, but this is not the preferred time for my Elephant. In the morning, my Elephant is sluggish and tries to convince my Rider that we can either delay until later or until tomorrow. My Rider knows this reluctance passes fairly soon but is a real deterrent most mornings. At this point, my Rider needs to employ tremendous leadership skills and encouragement. My Rider does several things to accomplish this:

1. I allow my Elephant to take it slowly [at first]. Pushing my Elephant too much will cause it to rebel, and run in the opposite direction, or cause it to become stubborn and sit down. I do this by getting up and going through a casual "waking up" routine of making my bed, getting dressed for exercise, walking to the exercise room, and starting my exercise with arm swings, squats, push-ups, sit-ups, etc. By this point, even though it is just 30 min since getting up, the Elephant is now participating in the activity and tends not to back out.
2. I do not try to fool the Elephant but rather ease him into the routine. Tricking the Elephant doesn't work and just builds distrust.
3. I remind the Elephant that we always feel great after the workout and that we have successfully completed the exercise routine many times. This is shaping the Path and encouragement for my Elephant. I tend to keep a very similar routine that my Elephant knows it can accomplish. Uncertainty can breed reluctance. My wife works out 6-7 days a week and does a number of different routines. Periodically, she invites me to participate in her routine, but this makes my Elephant skittish. I don't exercise because

I love to exercise. If I did, a variety of routines might be fun and interesting. I exercise because it is good for me and allows me to stay in shape—it is merely a means to an end. Keeping it simple and familiar is important for my Elephant.

4. I remind my Elephant that I allowed him to graze in the pasture and at times eat more than he should have. Now, to maintain our objectives, we need to include some short-term discomfort—no pain, no gain.
5. I listen to music or watch a TV show that my Elephant enjoys and even looks forward to. This makes the activity more enjoyable and helps the time to pass.
6. I keep my Elephant informed of progress throughout the routine. I'm specific about the exercises I do and the number of reps of each item. I include 30 min on the elliptical machine, varying resistance levels with specific time intervals that my Elephant knows it can achieve. My Elephant does better with exercise in stages. When he starts to get tired, my Rider allows him to look at the count-down timer to the end of the next interval. Breaking bigger tasks into smaller bite-size chunks keeps my Elephant from losing hope.

When the exercise is complete for another day, my Rider and Elephant invariably agree that it wasn't so bad. In fact, both feel good for the accomplishment and for persevering with a plan they know produces results.

For most, if not all, adopting intentionality involves a paradigm switch. It certainly was for me when it came to diet and exercise. I did not go on a diet. I literally had to change my eating and exercise habits and become much more intentional with habits that aligned with my objectives. Initially, to get to my desired weight, I had to be more strict and severe, but later, I was able to loosen up a little.

The point is this: If what you are currently doing accomplishes your objectives, then no change is necessary. However, if like most, and a large reason most of you are reading this book, you want something different—usually people want more: more consistency, more fulfillment, more results, etc.—and to get a different result, you need to do things differently than you have in the past. Everybody knows that continuing to do the same things over and over, yet expecting different results, is the definition of insanity.

For some, it's a matter of formulating a better plan, shaping the path, and/or truly committing to an already good plan. Directing your Rider is the first step. Second, you need to fuel the journey and give your Elephant the encouragement he needs to stay on the path.

The Elephant, Rider, and Path analogy is helpful to refer to when effecting or maintaining change.

NOTES AND TAKE-AWAYS

INTENTIONALITY ELEMENTS TO IMPLEMENT

CHAPTER 10

AWARENESS IS THE BEGINNING OF ALL LEARNING AND DEVELOPMENT

One of the great challenges in life is to know enough to think you're right, but not enough to realize you're wrong.

— NEIL DEGRASSE TYSON

I hate to break it to you. You've been lied to all these years. Ignorance is not bliss!

Ignorance might numb us from a reality that could be sad, disappointing, frustrating, and even harmful, but it's also ignorance that numbs us from experiencing freedom, release, knowledge, perspective, joy, connection, and even love.

It's the opposite of ignorance that allows us to learn, develop, and move forward in life. Awareness, not ignorance, is what ultimately leads to bliss. Awareness starts our journey to a better place and keeps us on a better path. Ignorance often leads us down the wrong path.

Awareness reveals options and possibilities. It's up to us to make better decisions and undertake better actions. That's why we all need mirrors in our lives to help us see what we otherwise would not see.

Mirrors are not just those shiny reflective pieces of glass that we strategically position in our bathrooms so that we can groom ourselves for others. Mirrors are a metaphor for anything that provides greater awareness—I can be a mirror for my wife after we have had a meal together and she wants to know if she has anything stuck in her teeth. Customer surveys are a form of mirror to gain insight into how well a business has served its patrons.

The challenge with the latter kind of mirror is accepting the awareness it provides at face value and using that information to forge improvements and change. Unfortunately, too many organizations have used the results of these surveys to keep score, rather than glean awareness of where things can be improved.

When a survey becomes a scorecard, rather than an awareness tool, the subject of the survey is tempted to coach the guest or team member to get a better score. Influencing the results of the survey is like bending the mirror.

Imagine if, after a meal, my wife asked if she had anything stuck in her teeth but prefaced the question with the suggestion that, if something was stuck in her teeth, it would make her feel less attractive, and it would hurt her feelings if I said there was something. What are the chances I would be a true mirror?

Years ago, I would go to the annual carnival in my hometown. I was always intrigued by the House of Mirrors. We would laugh when we saw our reflection in various bent mirrors. Some would make us look taller and thinner—that's the one I liked—while others made us look shorter and fatter. Yet others distorted our image and were funny to look at. Funny because we knew the reflection was not a true reflection.

Bending the mirror happens, for example, when customers are coached on how to fill out a survey or when we ask leading questions. In both cases, we are not allowing the mirror to be objective, but rather to tell us what we want to hear.

Bending the mirror only leads to a combination of ignorance and insanity. If we bend the mirror to provide us with a preferred [artificial] image, it keeps us from gaining awareness and making necessary changes.

The key to becoming our best is to intentionally avail ourselves of as many mirrors as possible and accept the awareness at face value. Then we need to decide which elements of awareness need to be acted upon and which elements just need to be accepted for the reflection it represents.

According to Henry Cloud, author of *The Power of the Other*, relationships are the most powerful mirrors we can benefit from. Using the metaphor of a computer, Cloud explains that while we all have a brain [the hardware] and a mind [the software], we need others [the developers] to develop our minds to full potential.

A Venn diagram provides a visual of how this works. Our potential is represented by the overlap of the three circles representing our brain, mind, and the input of others. Our brains [hardware] essentially stay constant while others provide feedback, awareness, information, and perspective to expand our minds, represented by the increase in the two circles to increase the size of the overlap and our potential.

A word of caution and a little insight. Not every relationship allows our minds to develop in a better manner. Good relationships expand our minds and bad relationships can, and usually do, have the effect of shrinking our minds and reducing our potential. You've heard it said that bad company corrupts good character.

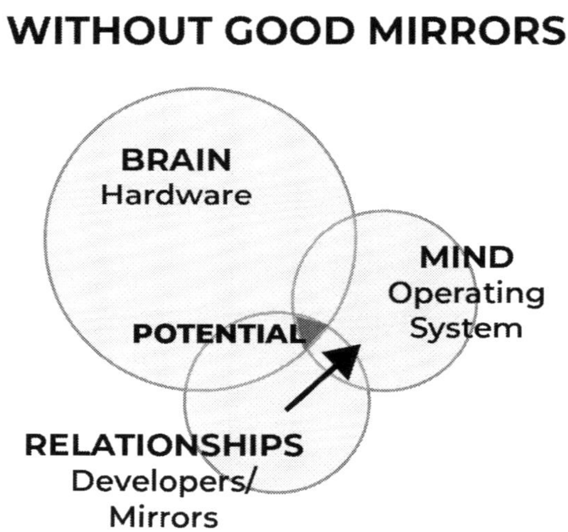

WITH GOOD MIRRORS

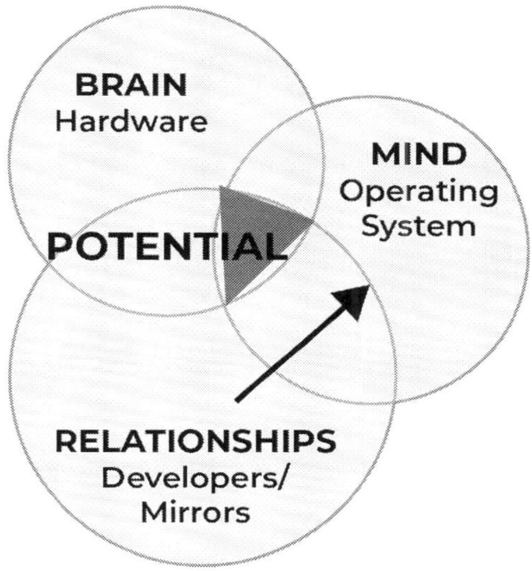

The reality is, however, that good relationships usually only take place when two or more people are willing to be transparent and vulnerable with each other. A lack of transparency and vulnerability leads to hazy, bent mirrors.

Great leaders recognize the value of accurate feedback. Hence, they humbly and actively engage mirrors so they can see what they otherwise cannot see and so they can tweak their situation until the reflection matches the image they are trying to create.

Most people are reluctant to share sensitive information for fear of hurting feelings or creating conflict. That's why great leaders learn to create a safe environment first. Then they invite and seek feedback in such a way that others are not only comfortable providing the feedback, but they feel like what they are going to share will be helpful to the leader. To do this, a good question for a leader to ask is, "What would you be willing to share with me that I may not want to hear, but I need to hear?"

This is inviting the other person to be candid and share in an open, honest, and helpful manner. Just because something is true doesn't mean it's helpful. For instance, telling somebody they are short may be true but not helpful. A good rule of thumb is to consider whether the insight is from something controllable or uncontrollable. People can't do anything about uncontrollable factors; hence, to share insights about an uncontrollable is not relevant nor helpful.

In her book, *Radical Candor*, Kim Scott provides insights into what candor is and how sharing candid feedback is beneficial to the hearer. Remember, as we learned above, we need each other to learn and grow. Without the insights provided by others, our development would be stunted, and we would not achieve our full potential.

Scott compares and contrasts four types of outcomes that arise from either sharing or withholding direct feedback in an environment of care or lack thereof. The four outcomes along with her model are:

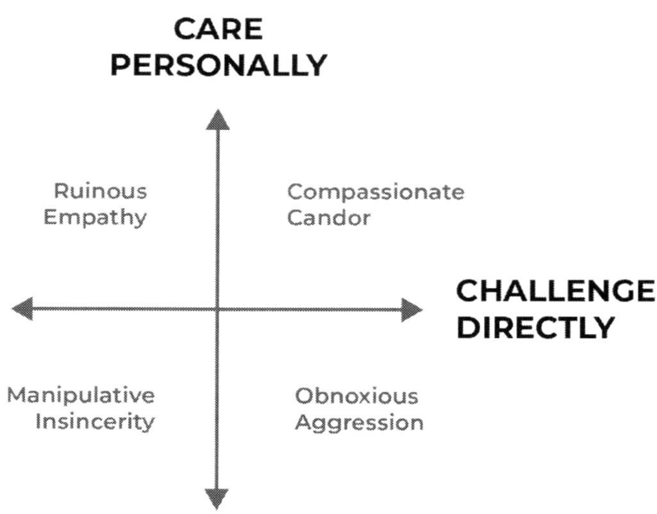

Obnoxious Aggression happens when somebody shares directly but without establishing a sense of care with the other person. In these cases, feedback can feel like an attack and can become obnoxious, especially if not invited.

Manipulative Insincerity happens when somebody doesn't care personally about somebody else and withholds important and relevant feedback from them. Many managers can fall into this trap when they share expectations but don't give praise and/or tell the person how they are doing.

Ruinous Empathy happens when somebody cares personally but withholds helpful information. It becomes ruinous because the person can get a false sense of reality, security, and confidence when they only hear positive or empathetic comments. Kids of parents who only give encouragement can grow up with this syndrome, which aligns with the research that high-performance teams operate in an environment of 3:1 positivity to negativity. Positivity is important, but it becomes disingenuous if not balanced with reality.

Compassionate Candor is helpful and happens when somebody cares personally and, therefore, recognizes that sharing certain critical insights is truly an act of caring.

That's why renowned Executive Coach, Marshall Goldsmith, author of *What Got You Here Won't Get You There*, suggests that providing feedback, and something he calls feed-forward, is a form of gift and should be received as such.

In speaking with a client one day, he said, "Let me be honest," to which I replied that I hoped he would always be honest and that a better expression might be, "Let me be candid." We discussed the concept of candor, and he appreciated the perspective. Since that conversation, he has mentioned a number of times how candor has become his new favorite word because of how candor improves communication.

NOTES AND TAKE-AWAYS

INTENTIONALITY ELEMENTS TO IMPLEMENT

CHAPTER 11

INTENTIONALITY FOR WHAT DOESN'T COME NATURALLY

Some things come natural, for everything else you need intentionality.

— MIKE RENTFRO

Every person is different. In fact, personalities can be like a fingerprint with slight or major nuances from person to person. Each personality is endowed with elements that come naturally, things we do almost without thought or effort, and elements that require a tremendous amount of effort and thought. That's why some people are better suited to undertake certain tasks or activities than other people.

Sure, most of us feel that we can do many, if not all, of the things that are identified as unnatural for us. The issue is not whether we can do those things; it's whether we are able to do those things well and for a sustained period, like we can with those things that come naturally.

Take public speaking for example. It's said that some people would rather die than speak in front of a large group of people. Interestingly, however, there are others, like me, who not only welcome public speaking opportunities but are energized by them.

Doing what comes naturally is typically energizing and results in far greater effectiveness and fulfillment than doing those things that don't come naturally. Unnatural tasks and activities drain our energy and result in frustration and long-term ineffectiveness.

That's why, in most circumstances, people eventually find their way to focus on doing what comes naturally, especially when it involves work and long-term relationships. We are drawn to situations and activities that energize us and are repelled by situations and activities that drain us. Unfortunately, for many, this journey to finding the right fit involves years, if not a lifetime, of trial and error.

During a coaching session with a client, I asked about one of his managers and how she was doing. My client spoke in positive terms about the great job the manager has been doing. He said she has been an incredible asset to the organization. I then asked if he had any concerns. His answer took me by surprise. He said that there was an issue that arose two years ago when he hired her that has been eating at him. I asked if he had ever brought the concern to her attention. He admitted that he had not. I asked why, and sheepishly, he confessed that he was afraid to ask at the time in case it would somehow scare her away from taking the job.

It's helpful to note that, based on my client's personality profile, it wasn't surprising that he shied away from addressing the concern. Challenge is not something that comes naturally to him. What comes naturally is smoothing over things, which is what he did for two years. Yet, it still clearly bothered him; otherwise, he would not have brought it up to me.

The good news is that I have a more dominant personality, and challenging situations comes naturally for me. It's not that I enjoy conflict or challenging others; it's just that I'm more willing to address things when I think it's important or helpful.

On this particular day, the manager shared how she felt he had been holding back approval from her, especially in the first year of her employment.

It's important for leaders to understand that healthy, connected people tend to reveal things to each other. They know that revealing clears the air and allows for an unencumbered environment. Concealing from each other, even little items, is felt by the other person and leads to disconnection.

I'm pleased to report that, in this situation, we were able to have a constructive conversation and clear the air on the issue that was bothering my client. And as is often the case in these situations, the manager was not aware there was an issue and would have easily dealt with the concern at the time had she been aware.

This is why celebrating and embracing the diversity of talents in teams is so powerful. None of us is good at everything, but when we combine diverse talents, we benefit from each other's strengths while filling in each other's weaknesses. But it requires humility on the side of the leader to admit an area of weakness to benefit from the other's strength.

Then there are people who get stuck in jobs that don't fit their natural bent. Why? In many cases, it's simply time and place, getting stuck in a job that was available and provided a paycheck. In other cases, we got stuck in a career, like law or medicine, because that was what others [parents] expected us to do.

The key to greater effectiveness and fulfillment is to understand how we are uniquely wired. This not only helps in the work environment, where teamwork is important and where performance is continuously measured, but in our personal lives where relationships are central to our well-being.

Many people stay in the wrong jobs or in poor relationships because they are afraid to venture out and try something else. Others have allowed their job or a relationship to dictate their path, rather than pursuing their passions. The fascinating thing is that passion and intrigue are often signals of things that are more aligned with our natural bent.

So, how does one discover their natural bent and avoid months, if not years, of unnecessary pain?

There are assessments available, backed by many years of research, that provide insights into how people are wired and what kinds of things are a better fit for them—things that ultimately provide them with a sense of inspiration and fulfillment.

One such assessment is the DiSC™. By answering a few questions, a person can learn whether their natural bent is more associated with Dominance, Influence, Steadiness, or Conscientiousness—hence the acronym DiSC™.

A DiSC™ assessment can be done online and in about 15 minutes, is relatively inexpensive, and results are immediately available. Most people find it uncanny how accurate these assessments are and how they reveal our natural bent.

At the heart of the assessment is the theory that there are two main drivers in all our lives, the degree to which we are outgoing versus reserved and the degree to which we prioritize tasks over people.

In the short term, we all have the same amount of time available—24 hours a day. Yet, because time is limited, we are all forced to prioritize how we invest that time. We have the propensity to do things that align with our natural bent, which are also typically the things that energize us. On the other hand, as noted above, while we can often do things that do not come naturally for us, these unnatural activities, tasks, or behaviors tend to drain us. Hence, if we are honest with ourselves and listen to our gut feeling, we will be more apt to follow a path that aligns with our personalities or what we are hard-wired to do.

The interesting thing is that what comes naturally for one person may be the polar opposite of what comes naturally to another person. For instance, while meeting new people and engaging in small talk is energizing for one person, say a typical salesperson, it can be draining for another, like an accountant. At the same time, crunching numbers and organizing documents may be energizing for one person, an accountant, and draining for another, a salesperson.

Many resources are available for those who want to take advantage of this powerful tool. All you need to do is search the Internet for DiSC™ Assessments. There are some that are even available for free but be aware that you often get what you pay for.

One of the more popular tools is called Everything DiSC™, published by John Wiley and Sons, Inc., which provides numerous in-depth reports that produce a dot on a graph to pinpoint your natural personality style. The typical report is 27 pages, which tells your story in the first seven pages to expand self-awareness and another twenty pages of reference materials to provide insights into how to interact better with other personality types.

The following graphic provides an overview of the DiSC™ Model.

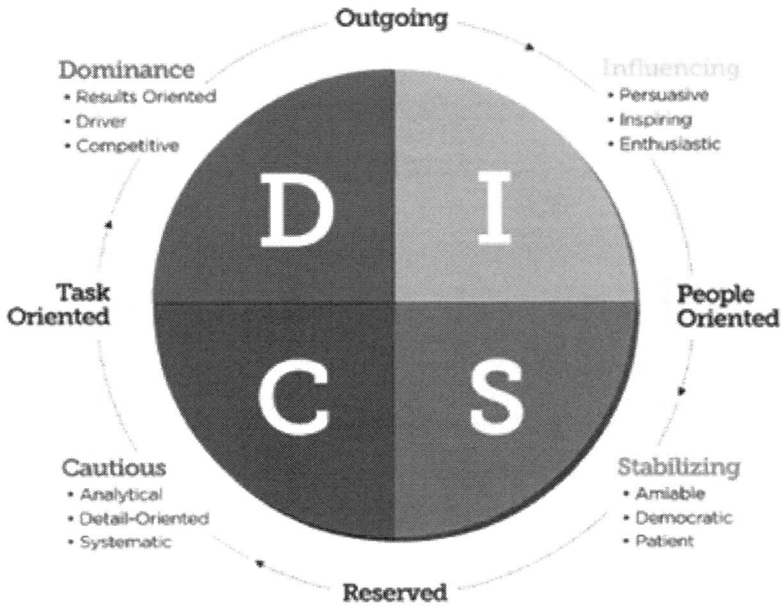

All "dots" reside somewhere within this graphic and are associated with a particular style of personality—representing things that we like, prefer, and prioritize. In other words, the assessment identifies in an objective manner what kinds of things come naturally for each personality style.

While dots tend to fit nicely into one of the four quadrants, the actual representation of a personality style is much more fluid. Think of it more like a color spectrum that has a blending of the four colors that make up this graphic.

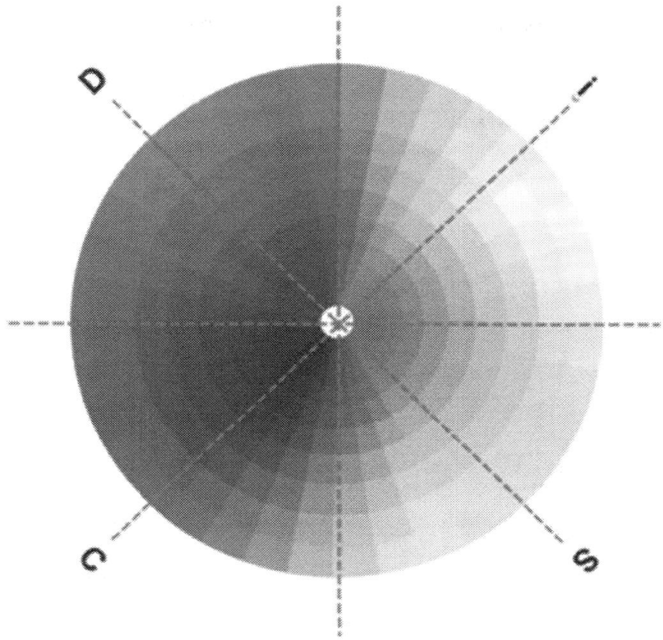

Hence, rather than seeing this as four distinctly different personality styles, think of it as thousands of personality variations within four general categories.

The premise is that no dot, or personality style, is better than any other dot, or personality style. The relevance and effectiveness of each dot is in how it is applied in any given situation or how it impacts on what is to be accomplished. For instance, an **i** [Influencer] style is often associated with people in sales—where there is a benefit from being more outgoing and more people-focused. Compare this to a **C** [Conscientious] style, which is often associated with people in accounting—where there is benefit from being more reserved and task-focused.

A general overview of each of the four categories, is:
Dominance [D]:

- Direct
- Firm
- Strong-willed
- Forceful
- Results-oriented

Influence [i]:

- Outgoing
- Enthusiastic
- Optimistic
- High-spirited
- Lively

Steadiness [S]:

- Even-tempered
- Accommodating
- Patient
- Humble
- Tactful

Conscientiousness [C]:

- Analytical
- Reserved
- Precise
- Private
- Systematic

To provide an immediate and simple sense of each of these personalities, authors Gary Smalley and John Trent, in their book *The Treasure Tree: Helping Kids Understand Their Personality*, suggest that nature provides examples of the four personality styles in the following animals:

Dominance—A Lion
Influencer—An Otter
Steadiness—A Golden Retriever
Conscientiousness—A Beaver

The Everything DiSC™ tool also identifies eight different priorities that each person exhibits and the degree to which each of these priorities is natural for that individual:

- Drive [for results]
- Action
- Encouragement
- Collaboration
- Support
- Reliability
- Objectivity
- Challenge

One objection that I often hear when reviewing DiSC™ profiles with clients is the priority chart. Many express concern that it isn't accurate because it suggests that certain elements for them are low.

The point of the priority chart is to show you what comes naturally and what doesn't come as naturally. The reality is that you can do virtually anything you want, but you need to be honest with yourself and realize that, while you can do things that seem less natural, doing those things requires much greater intentionality and that intentionality takes much more energy to sustain than something that comes more naturally. That is why the unnatural things are more draining because they take more energy. Refer to the example above of the typical salesperson and accountant.

The challenge in life is that we are a blending of many influences, opportunities, and experiences that have shaped our lives and paths. That is why making life and career choices can be so challenging.

We tend to be a blending of the following six types of people:

- Who we think we are—self-image.
- Who others think we are—public perception.
- Who we are at work—we all wear work masks to fit in and keep our jobs.
- Who we are at home—where we can relax and be more of ourselves, yet restricted or impacted by the other personalities in our household.
- Who we are under stress. This is a wildcard because stress impacts people in very different ways and for very different reasons. That being said, the impact of stress is beyond the scope of this book.
- Who we really are. This is the most important person to understand because that is the person who will feel the most inspired and fulfilled while achieving the best outcomes. The challenge is getting insights that are objective and unbiased, which typically only come from science-based and research-validated assessments.

So, the main benefit of personality profiling is to help people better understand themselves, what comes naturally, to gain confidence in following a path that better aligns with who they really are and are best suited to doing, and ultimately to be able to achieve better sustainable results. A secondary benefit is in how we gain a better understanding of other people and why they do the things they do. Knowing ourselves is important, but knowing others is also important if we are to build more productive relationships and work more effectively in teams.

A challenge associated with not knowing others is something called the Fundamental Attribution Error, which is a clinical term for how we judge people incorrectly when we don't know them. An example usually helps explain how this works.

Imagine it's a Sunday afternoon, and you are driving down a two-lane road, one lane in each direction, on your way to visit a friend in the hospital. There is a fair amount of traffic, but it's moving along well.

Suddenly, you notice in your rearview mirror a vehicle approaching quickly from behind. At first, you fear it might collide with you, but instead, it pulls up close and maintains a very close distance behind you. For the next few moments, the vehicle veers to the left multiple times while maintaining a close distance. As soon as a gap in the oncoming traffic presents itself, the vehicle speeds past you and cuts you off in the process.

At the moment when the vehicle cuts you off, what is your immediate impression of the other driver?

If you are like most people, you'll suggest the other driver is an ass or something worse. In this kind of situation, it's normal to feel a degree of emotion and react with a negative opinion.

As you process what just happened, you continue your drive to the hospital. Upon arriving at the hospital, you notice the vehicle that cut you off is there at the front of the hospital parked at the doors to the emergency ward.

Does the added information change your perspective about the other driver?

Now you're curious. After finding a parking spot, you walk in the front of the emergency ward and ask a nurse about the vehicle parked out front. The nurse shares how a father brought in his son who fell from a tree and had multiple injuries. How are you feeling about the driver now that you know even more?

Don't feel bad. We all fall into the Fundamental Attribution Error when we don't know others and the motives behind what we perceive to be negative actions. Even Abraham Lincoln once said, "I really don't like that person. I think I need to get to know them better."

The essence of the Fundamental Attribution Error is that, when we don't know somebody, we falsely attribute negative actions to a person's character—they are a jerk—and positive outcomes to their environment—they were lucky.

On the flip side, when it comes to us and people we know, we naturally attribute negative outcomes to the environment and positive actions to our character.

We tend to attribute the opposite to people we know. That's why it's so important to get to know people, so we can more appropriately assess their actions.

That's also why it's so important to do a good job of onboarding new staff into our organizations. Otherwise, imagine how they might be judged incorrectly by those with whom they need to work closely, while the new hire also assesses others incorrectly.

A good practice is to attribute positive intent to all people, especially when we don't have all the facts.

NOTES AND TAKE-AWAYS

INTENTIONALITY ELEMENTS TO IMPLEMENT

SECTION TWO

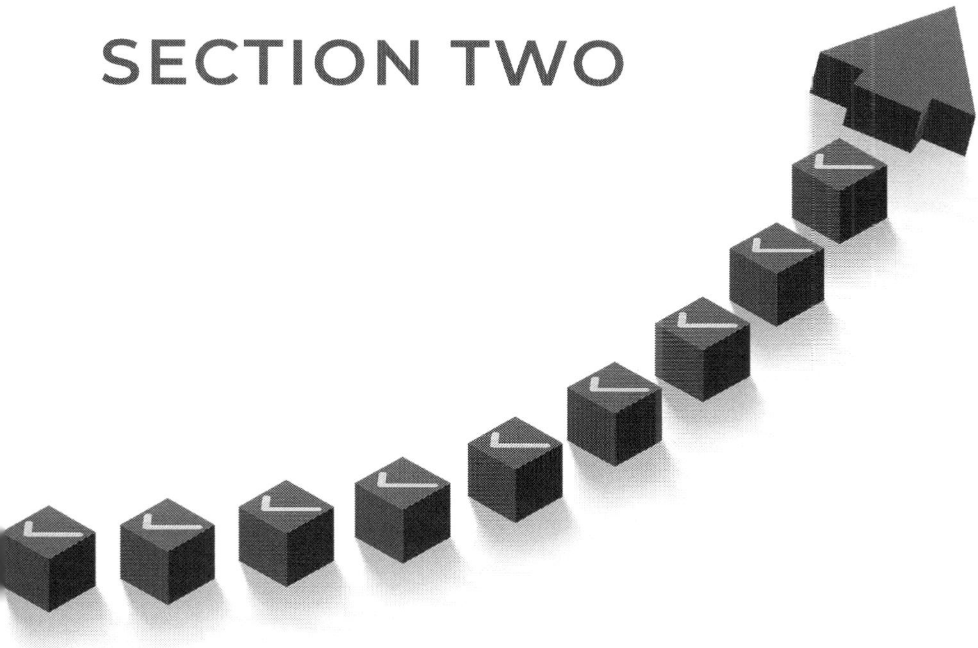

THE INTENTIONALITY MODEL

CHAPTER 12

THE MODEL

Words may inspire, but only ACTION creates change. Most of us live our lives by accident–we live life as it happens. Fulfillment comes when we live our lives on purpose.

— SIMON SINEK

Oftentimes it's better to be reminded than instructed.

— SAMUEL L. JOHNSON

I'm not under the illusion that what I'm going to present is new information as much as it may be a new way of presenting the information such that maybe you connect with it seemingly for the first time. That is the essence of an epiphany.

I'm convinced that, unless we can connect with information in such a way that we are able to internalize it, we are unlikely to incorporate it into our lives.

Above I shared the story of the penny. While we may not all be given the choice between a million dollars and a penny, we all have at least a penny to start with and a certain amount of time in which to multiply our penny. The challenge, and opportunity, is in making better choices leading to better actions. So there really are no acceptable excuses for not getting on a better path to success. The battle we all rage daily is with our elephant, who is short-sighted and wants to take the easy path.

In the Bible, the apostle Paul lamented, "I do not understand what I do. For what I want to do I do not do, but what I hate I do." (Romans 7:15 NIV)

The Intentionality Model depicts the theory behind taking positive actions that are as easy to do as not to do and that keep us on our trajectory to the results we seek, versus taking negative actions or simply choosing to do nothing.

THE INTENTIONALITY MODEL

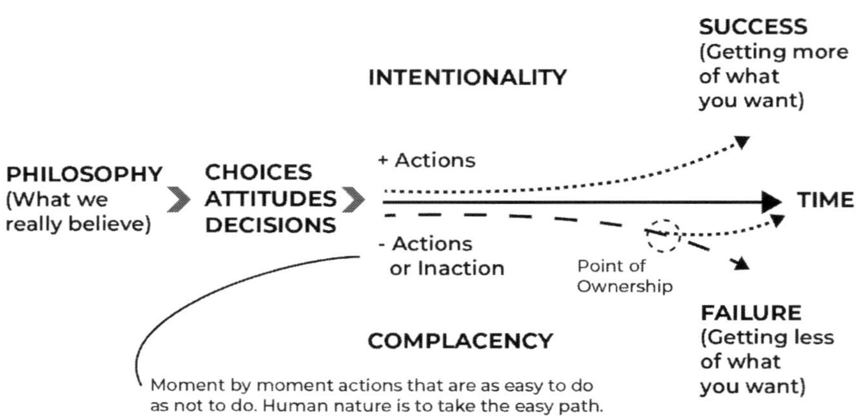

(© Mast 2023)

Depending on how we string together our positive and negative actions determines the results we ultimately reap.

Consistently taking positive action will result in more success, or greater results, while less consistency with positive actions, or even greater consistency with negative actions, will lead to less success or even failure, depending on what you are trying to achieve.

The fundamental principle of intentionality is that positive actions tend to lead to positive results, and negative actions, or even inaction, lead to diminished or negative results. In a manner of speaking, by following a practice of intentionality, results are virtually guaranteed. The challenge is that positive actions are as easy to do as they are not to do, but we don't always feel like doing what we should.

Unfortunately, as you will discover below, human nature tends toward complacency and inaction, ultimately leading to poorer results. Hence, intentionality is all about taking intentional positive action, guided by our philosophy, and countering human nature moment by moment.

Here's an example. A health-conscious person has the option of riding the elevator or walking the stairs. Riding the elevator is not a bad thing, but it will not provide as much exercise as walking the stairs does.

I would guess that, in 80% of the situations, taking the stairs can be as quick, if not quicker, than taking the elevator. Yet, in this everyday example, most people take the elevator, even to travel between single floors, not even considering stairs as an option. Yet, many of those same people secretly wish they could lose a few pounds.

The elevator has become second nature, and most don't even give it any thought. It's there, easy, and represents the path of least resistance. An intentionality-minded person, on the other hand, is always considering available options and doing those things that align with their philosophy—beliefs, values, and goals.

Knowing is not doing. We all know that exercise is good for our bodies and leads to better health. We also know that we generally don't get enough regular exercise. Further, most people are also aware that heart disease (which is the number one killer of Americans – CDC https://www.cdc.gov/nchs/products/databriefs/db355.htm) can be reduced by exercising more. Yet, our nature [elephant] is complacent, enjoys convenience, and squanders time and opportunity.

A practice of intentionality keeps us more conscious of our present and future reality and the options available. A mindset of intentionality causes us to be much more conscious of our situation and to take better actions, especially when those actions are as easy to do as not to do.

Intentionality requires moment-by-moment consciousness and commitment and, in many cases, the will to overcome our emotional elephant (more on this below).

The Intentionality Model can be broken down into the following key components, for which I will give a brief introduction and then later expand further:

- Time
- Philosophy
- Choices and Attitudes
- Positive Actions, Negative Actions, and Inaction
- Consequences and Results

Time: In theory, we all have the same amount of time (24/7) and the same opportunity to make choices and act during that time. Certainly, I realize that we all experience different circumstances during our time, but for the sake of the model and what we can learn from it, let's agree that we have the same amount of time allocated to us and the same opportunities to choose what we are going to do with the time we have.

The key to intentionality is making better use of the time available to us. To do so, we need to be more conscious of the choices we make and the actions we take. The challenge tends not to be with the big and/or urgent things. We can usually get our Rider and Elephant working together on those. The challenge is with small choices and actions—those that seem less urgent and less significant—because they are usually as easy to do as they are not to do.

Not much more needs to be said about time, as it is a straightforward concept, except maybe to provide a reminder that every squandered second is lost forever. Those who accomplish the most recognize each second is like a penny that can compound into big results if invested well over a longer period. The challenge is that we rarely see the results of those investments at the time we are making them.

Philosophy: The following diagram provides further scientific insights into how two significant parts of our brain, the Neocortex (rational brain) and Limbic (emotional brain), affect what we do and why we do it.

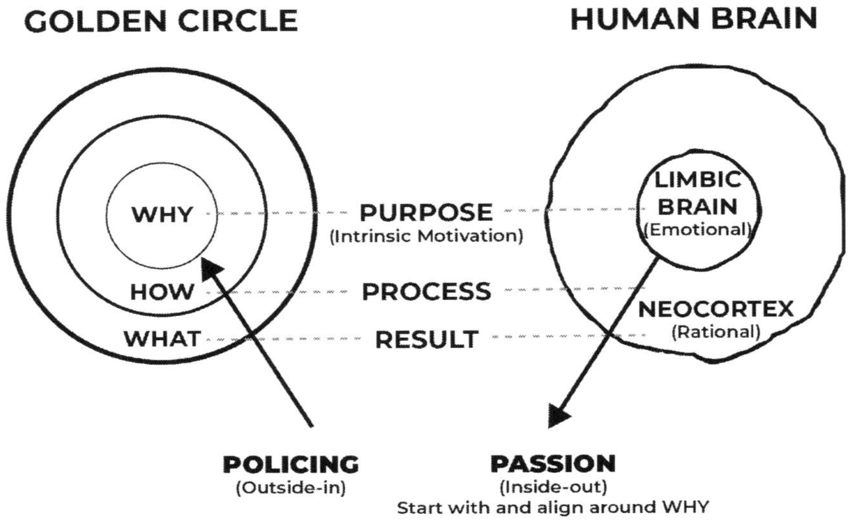

In his book, *Start with Why*, Simon Sinek explains how people don't buy what you do (rational), rather they buy why you do it (emotional). It's just like the Rider (rational brain) and the Elephant (emotional brain) (see analogy above).

Sinek talks about the importance of having a sense of purpose to drive our actions and how the most effective teams are connected through a common purpose and shared values.

When it comes to teams, it is all about direction, alignment, and engagement. That's why the Intentionality Model starts with a need for clarity around philosophy.

Merriam-Webster defines philosophy, amongst other things, as, "The most basic beliefs, concepts, and attitudes of an individual or group." I like to simplify the definition to, "What we really believe," which is observed through the actions we take.

It's not just what we believe, which would be summed up by the words we use to describe our beliefs, but by what we really believe, which is observed in the actions we take. Remember the three frogs on a log from the introduction? It's not enough that one decides to jump. With no action, there is no result.

Choices, Decisions, and Attitudes: The precursor to our actions tends to be our thought process, which is made up of our choices and attitudes, which are guided by our philosophy. This is why clarity of and consistent commitment to our philosophy is so important.

Even though we make many poor choices and often have bad attitudes, causing us to get off track, our philosophy is the North Star or beacon that guides our way and brings us back.

Every person and every team need clarity around their philosophy and what their non-negotiables are. You only have one life to live, so you need to make the most of it.

Deep down, all of us have some sense of the values we consider to be core to our being. It is when we compromise our core values that we demonstrate a lack of integrity.

We often use words like honesty and integrity interchangeably, but they are very different concepts. A thief, by definition, breaks the law and is dishonest when she steals something. However, she is operating with integrity when she steals something because that is what thieves do.

In contrast, a judge who has sworn to uphold the law is not only dishonest but operating without integrity if she were to steal something.

It's been said that trying to please everybody is the key to failure. But if we have not defined and we are not committed to core values, it's easy to lose our way. Yes, taking one path means we don't take another path, but that is the whole point. We need to maintain a steady course toward our beacon. It's about the compounding effect of better actions. That's what we learned from the penny story.

The starting point in all of this is to define the values by which you as an individual, or a team, commit to living. Once defined, these values need to be top of mind so they can guide individual and team behaviors moment by moment, day by day, month by month, and year by year. This is something the leaders at Chick-fil-A have done well over the years—defining values, committing to live the values, hiring people using core values as a filter, and holding everybody, including the leaders, accountable to living and operating in line with the values.

Choices affect direction and attitudes affect momentum.

Positive Actions, Negative Actions, and Complacency:

There are several reasons for our inaction or our slowness to act.

1. **We are all procrastinators.** Many people live by this mantra, especially when it comes to things that are less enjoyable to do: *Why do anything today that can be put off until tomorrow?* Motivation is a major factor when it comes to procrastination. We almost always have time for fun things, like playing golf, but put off the less fun activities, like cleaning the garage. A few ways to apply intentionality to counteract procrastination include:
    - Break the task into smaller chunks that can be completed in less time, less energy, and with minimal disruption to our schedule. Instead of trying to tackle the entire garage in one Saturday, pick a small task, like cleaning up your workbench, which will only take about an hour. The fascinating reality is that, once we overcome our reluctance threshold and start the task, we often get motivated to do more than we thought we would.
    - Establish habits that cause more of your behaviors to become a natural part of your daily, weekly, or monthly

rhythm. For example, most people brush their teeth at the same time each day and don't need to remind themselves—they either do it as part of their morning or evening routines, or they do so after each meal. Another example is doing laundry or paying bills—most choose a specific day and time each week, knowing the activity is critical to the proper functioning of their other activities. An interesting fact is that habits are especially effective in controlling the Elephant because the activity tends to bypass the normal brain functions relating to motivation and willpower.

- Ask somebody to touch base with you at agreed intervals and hold you accountable. Many people know their Elephant is a bully and need the assistance of others to motivate them to take action.

2. **We hope [falsely] in the future, but do not change anything today.** In other words, we are merely giving lip service to the things we want if we don't act. Hope is a good thing because it props us up with positivity as we go through difficult times. False hope, however, has no basis in reality and usually just delays the inevitable disappointment. Just like the definition of insanity, hoping for a different result without making changes is false hope or a dream. Hope is only helpful when we are in the middle of new action, and we need the additional encouragement to stay the course. If I start a new exercise routine to lose weight, get into better physical shape, and improve my health, I hope my efforts will deliver results that are helpful to stay the course. If, on the other hand, I step on the scale in the morning,

hoping it shows a lower number, but I don't change any of my eating and exercise habits, that is false hope.

3. **Gravity and the second law of thermodynamics (the scientific fact that everything is decaying) are working against us.** This topic is covered in more detail later, but for now, it is helpful to understand that the only way to counteract the natural downward pull [of life] is to intentionally move in an upward [positive] direction toward our objectives.

4. **Lack of self-awareness and unintended consequences.** Humility and emotional intelligence both require a high degree of self-awareness. The reality is that all of us lack self-awareness to some degree. And those who believe they are the most self-aware are probably the ones that lack it the most. Neil DeGrasse Tyson captured the essence of why a lack of self-awareness can be an issue when he said, "One of the great challenges in life is knowing enough to think you're right, but not enough to know you're wrong." The good news for those who lack self-awareness is that there is always "other awareness." Unfortunately, to seek and accept feedback from others, we need a high degree of humility. So, how do you know if you lack self-awareness if you don't have self-awareness? Great question. Ignorance is bliss, right? No, wrong.

Two indicators of a lack of self-awareness include: 1) your efforts are not producing the kind of results that you want, and you don't know what to do differently, and/or 2) others are constantly giving you feedback you don't want to hear.

5. **Lack of inspiration.** Inspiration is a form of motivation. It is the kind that comes from within. Others play a role in our inspiration much like a farmer plays a role in the harvest. Inspiration is like a seed that grows and results in a crop. The farmer plants and nurtures the seed but cannot force it to grow. There are two main categories of motivation: internal and external. Scientifically, these are referred to as intrinsic and extrinsic motivation. Inspiration is a form of intrinsic motivation, which research shows accounts for 30% to 60% of our drive. Dan Pink, in his book *Drive*, shows that the biggest factors that generate intrinsic motivation are:

    Autonomy: Directing our own steps and path.

    Mastery: Getting better at something.

    Purpose: Being part of a larger cause that is worth fighting for.

Consequences and Results:

All actions have consequences and produce a result, whether positive or negative, intended, or unintended. Foundational principles of science suggest that forces are always acting on matter and that equilibrium is only achieved when equal and opposite forces are present. Inertia says that a body at rest tends to stay at rest, and a body in motion tends to stay in motion. When equal and opposite forces are pushing on a body, it will tend not to move, but when one of the forces pushes harder than another, the body tends to move in the direction of the force. This suggests there are always consequences to the force of our actions.

Unintended consequences happen when we push in a direction, we believe to be correct only to learn later that the direction was not correct. Most do not intend to go in the wrong direction, but as they do, their actions result in [unintended] consequences.

The Intentionality Model shows how many small positive actions result in many small [intentional] positive consequences and multiply like the penny towards success over time. In the same way, many small poor choices and actions, or lack of positive actions, or even inaction, result in many small [unintentional] negative consequences and multiply towards failure over time.

The challenge in the short term is that we often do not see a measurable difference in consequences between small positive actions compared with small negative actions. Multiplied over time, however, the subtle different consequences of these actions, like with the penny, result in very different outcomes.

While many small poor choices and actions, or lack of positive actions, or even inaction, result in many small [unintentional] negative consequences and multiply towards failure over time, that failure is rarely fatal. Failure with respect to intentionality simply suggests our trajectory is off course and will not hit our intended target or objective. The good news is that, after recognizing when you're off course, you simply need to own the fact that you are off course and make course corrections to set a trajectory that will move you in the right direction. That's why awareness is so important. Without awareness, you may not know when you're off course until course corrections are too difficult or impossible to make.

Philosophy is the beacon that guides our actions and keeps us on the right path. It's not just about what we believe, but what we truly believe, which is the subject of the next chapter.

NOTES AND TAKE-AWAYS

INTENTIONALITY ELEMENTS TO IMPLEMENT

CHAPTER 13

PHILOSOPHY FIRST

One's philosophy is not best expressed in words; it is expressed in the choices one makes... and the choices we make are ultimately our responsibility.

— ELEANOR ROOSEVELT

Knowing is not doing. Just because we believe something does not mean we will do something.

Most people are quick to tell you what they believe. However, words are cheap and typically do not produce results by themselves. Results only come through actions.

The way to know what a person truly believes is to look at their actions. Their actions tell the story of what they truly believe or the philosophy that acts as a guiding principle for their behavior.

Hence, the first step in putting intentionality into practice is to capture the essence of an individual's or team's philosophy in words. This can take many forms, such as a statement of philosophy, a culture statement, or the introduction to a playbook.

Most people think about these kinds of things at different times in their lives, especially when their current efforts are not proving successful, but they do not take the time to write them down. That's a pity and a big factor that no doubt contributes to their struggles.

Everybody operates from an underlying philosophy that determines most of what they do and why they do it. So, the way to move forward in a more positive manner is to write out your philosophy and assess whether your current mindset will get you to where you want to go.

This is the approach intentional individuals take. They recognize the value and importance of working through their thoughts and writing down a formal vision, mission, and values statement. The act of writing it down forces greater reflection, clarity, and internalization and thereby results in greater commitment and consistency.

If you have not previously done this exercise, now would be a great time to start. Consider putting a bookmark right here and turning to Appendix A, where there is a simple format for writing out your philosophy.

Think of your vision, mission, and values statements as your owner's manual. Unfortunately, most people adopt the saying, "If at first you don't succeed, try again." Others live by the mantra, "If at first you don't succeed, read the owner's manual." The intentionality approach is to read the owner's manual first and follow the steps suggested by the manufacturer, inventor, creator, designer, etc.

Since individuals only need to direct themselves, a formal approach like that outlined in Appendix A, while advisable, may seem extreme to most individuals, so they don't do it. Remember, intentionality is about doing the little things that are as easy not to do as they are to do.

Once you get two or more people together, the exercise of defining and writing out philosophy and guiding principles becomes exponentially more important. That is why intentional organizations spend time defining their vision, mission, and values so as to align their team around a common purpose and code of conduct.

Unfortunately, too many of these statements of philosophy remain just words, or good intentions, and only impact near-term efforts. Many are akin to writing out New Year's resolutions or creating marketing materials that are handed out or hung on the wall.

As cited in a *Forbes Health* article, March 9, 2023, New Year's Resolution Statistics 2023, failing at New Year's resolutions is so common that there's even a slew of (unofficial) dates commemorating such failures—some sources cite "Ditch New Year's Resolutions Day" as January 17 while others denote the second Friday in January as "Quitter's Day."

I "discovered" intentionality during the early stages of a weight loss effort.

Ironically, on December 30th, 2011, as I was recovering from having eaten too much good food at Thanksgiving and during Christmas, I was contemplating what the second half of my life would be like. I would be turning 50 in July 2012, and at that very moment, I was literally feeling fed-up.

While I seldom made, let alone wrote out, New Year's resolutions. If asked at the end of 2011 what my New Year's resolution was, I could have told you that I would love to lose a few pounds. But that was a fleeting thought. My words suggested a philosophy of physical fitness, but my past actions told a different story.

At the time, I was 49 years old and 50 pounds overweight. The good food at Thanksgiving and during Christmas that year had only added a few more pounds, but those were the pounds that tipped the mental scale for me. The first forty-five excess pounds had slowly accumulated over the prior twenty-five years.

It's amazing how things like weight and debt can creep up on us over time. But as easy as it creeps up, it should be to slough off, right? Sure, in theory, but if it was that easy, everybody would just do it.

Keep reading if you find losing weight or accomplishing other objectives is not as easy as reminding yourself to just do it.

What I learned on my weight-loss journey is that losing weight and keeping it off can be relatively easy with a practice of intentionality. My hope is that you will discover what it means to live with intentionality and that you will enjoy greater fulfillment by understanding and internalizing the art and science of just doing it.

NOTES AND TAKE-AWAYS

INTENTIONALITY ELEMENTS TO IMPLEMENT

CHAPTER 14

TRAJECTORY

You Should be far more concerned with your current trajectory than with your current results.

— JAMES CLEAR

Earlier I suggested that the precursor to our actions is our thought process, which is made up of our choices and attitudes guided by our philosophy. This is why clarity around our philosophy is so important.

Above, I also mentioned how time, choices, and attitudes play a role in the Intentionality Model. Here I want to focus on action, inaction, and the concept of trajectory.

One way to understand the concept of trajectory is to envision an arrow like in the diagram on the next page:

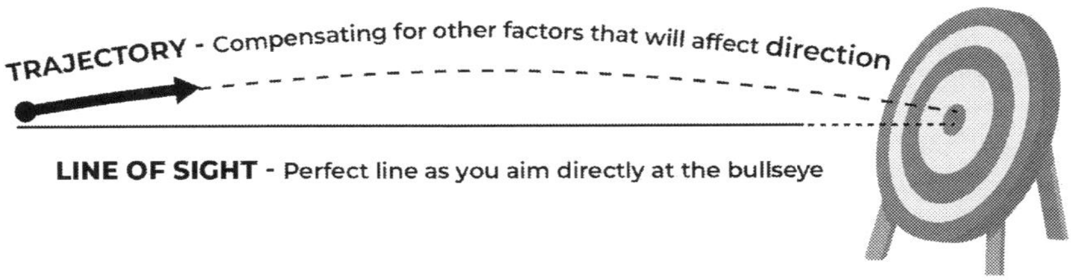

For an arrow to hit its target, the archer needs to set the arrow on a trajectory that takes into account the distance from the target, the speed at which the arrow will fly, launch angle, and the other forces that will affect the arrow, like gravity and wind, as it flies. Trajectory is essentially the path along which the arrow will fly given all the factors that affect the arrow's flight.

Trajectory is an important concept, especially when we are not able to intervene in the process once the object has been released, like in the case of the arrow. Mathematicians have formulated complex formulas and algorithms to predict where the arrow will end up given the forces that are acting on it along the way.

Imagine how complex the algorithms would be for a rocket that needs to fly that much farther. What scientists have learned is the value of intervention at strategic times to assist the rocket in changing course and putting it on a different trajectory based on feedback during flight.

Airplanes almost always reach their destination because they fly on safe, effective trajectories. At the start of a flight, all pilots, whether weekend sojourners or commercial professionals, are required to formulate a flight plan, considering as many known factors as possible. During flight, pilots are required to fly toward specific beacons. If the plane goes off track more than a few degrees from the line of sight between beacons, the pilot hears a pinging sound to alert the pilot to adjust to get the plane back on course.

Arrows, rockets, and planes rely on accurate trajectories to reach their desired destination. In all cases, these moving objects are adversely affected by factors that serve to detract it from its course.

In the context of trajectory, let me introduce you to the 2nd Law of Thermodynamics and the concept of entropy. I realize this sounds like something discussed on an episode of the hit TV show *The Big Bang Theory*.

While I want to tie in the science behind why intentionality holds the key to achieving better results, I also want to be careful not to dive too deep into the science and lose readers in the process. I am intentionally trying to keep this simple. There are many good resources available to anyone wanting to dig deeper into this complex subject.

2ND LAW OF THERMODYNAMICS

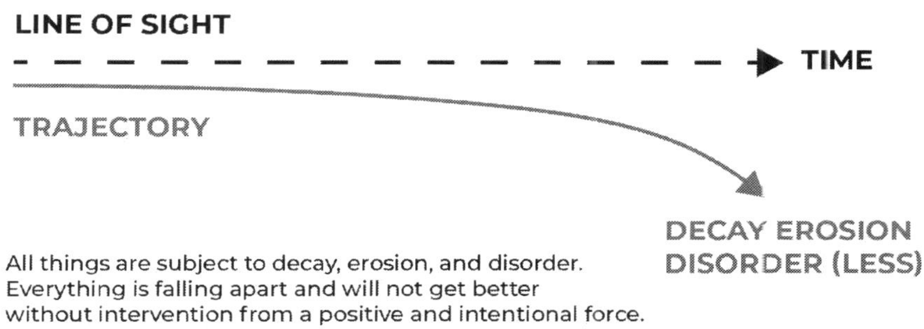

For our purposes, the key takeaway is that the 2nd Law of Thermodynamics speaks to the idea that everything in the world is decaying and left to its own vices, tends to disorder. Conceptually, gravity provides a simple metaphor for how the 2nd Law of Thermodynamics affects human nature and action.

Where gravity provides a downward pull on all objects on the earth, the 2nd Law of Thermodynamics explains why everything tends toward disarray, disorder, and decay.

A jigsaw puzzle serves to provide a helpful example. Imagine opening a new box of 1,000 jigsaw puzzle pieces and dumping the pieces on the ground. Do you anticipate and expect that, when you do so, the puzzle will land on the floor all put together in the correct order? Of course not. We fully anticipate that what lands on the floor (due to gravity) is 1,000 puzzle pieces with no sense of order at all. Some pieces will be upside down, while others will be facing in the wrong direction, etc.

We also fully anticipate that the puzzle will require our intervention to place the pieces exactly where they need to go. In fact, that is exactly the reason we purchased the puzzle, to undertake the challenge of putting the puzzle together. Those who enjoy a challenge find it to be fun and a great way to pass the time.

For our purposes, think of entropy as the measure of disorder. Sure, the box of pieces could fall perfectly in order when dumped on the floor, but entropy suggests the chances are exponentially greater that it will not. Mathematically, there is the possibility that the pieces fall in perfect order to create the completed picture, but there is an astronomical number of combinations where the pieces land on the floor totally out of order.

Even Murphy's Law reminds us that, *Anything that can go wrong, will go wrong.*

Mathematically speaking, an orderly outcome is incredibly unlikely to happen at random—James Clear, Entropy: *Why Life Always Seems to Get More Complicated.* (https://jamesclear.com/entropy)

So, why is this so relevant to our discussion here? The core concept here is that nothing in the world is getting better on its own. Everything is decaying and dying, and without intervention, the natural result is death and chaos.

Appropriate and timely intervention is the key to following a trajectory to success. Without intervention, most trajectories will lead to failure due to the destructive effect (downward pull) of the 2nd Law of Thermodynamics.

This is why leadership is so important to the success of teams. Leaders inspire and facilitate intentional action or intentionality. In this context, I define leadership as intentional influencing—to help a team navigate from here to there.

Look again at the diagram above. Hopefully, it makes more sense now. The reason intentional action, or intentionality, together with leadership, is so relevant is that, without these two elements, our lives would be a mess. Everything would follow the downward curve.

At the same time, intentionality and leadership offer hope that, with appropriate and timely intervention, we can follow the upper curve and achieve remarkable positive outcomes.

NOTES AND TAKE-AWAYS

INTENTIONALITY ELEMENTS TO IMPLEMENT

CHAPTER 15

CONSISTENCY OVER INTENSITY

Greatness is not born from one success. Greatness is born from persevering through the countless failed attempts that preceded.

— SIMON SINEK

Aesop's fable about *The Tortoise and the Hare* has taught children for centuries that slow and steady wins the race. This is central to intentionality as well.

We live in a 'now' society and therefore tend to be intense people. We favor immediate gratification over waiting and are willing to pay more to get what we want now. It's hard to fend off the urges of our Elephant. The Rider has a limited amount of willpower and must use every tool available to him to stay the course for long-term success.

Intensity is a great trait for those things we need to get done now. The challenge is that intensity is not the solution for everything. Think about individuals who are overweight and want to lose a few pounds. The weight did not build up on the body overnight and cannot typically be shed overnight. An intense person may opt for surgery, but that is a severe and expensive option with a number of potential side-effects.

There are many things we do daily to maintain good health and well-being: like sleeping, eating, exercising, brushing our teeth, etc. We do these things in relatively small amounts or for short periods of time every day. It would seem silly to think that we can brush our teeth for an hour on the first day of each month instead of doing so each day for two minutes. Intuitively, in these situations, we know that frequency is better than intensity. So, we build brushing our teeth into a daily habit and don't have to give it much thought. Whether in the morning, the evening, or both, or after every meal, we have established mental triggers that signal when we need to brush our teeth, and we just do it.

Habits and triggers are important elements in making intentionality work.

More than anything, we need to trust the process of intentionality and take little steps regularly and consistently over a longer period. For example, when we purchase a house, we trust that, if we make our monthly payment, we will pay off our mortgage and own the house outright after 30 years. Fortunately, financial institutions have made homeownership possible by providing immediate funds, but we need to stay committed to our monthly mortgage payments if we want to keep our home.

The key to losing weight is not a temporary diet but a change in eating habits where the new habits introduce a lower caloric intake than what is required to maintain a certain body weight.

Simply reversing bad eating habits is a good first step. Stop doing the things that led to the gaining of excess weight in the first place.

Exercise is also a great element when it comes to losing or maintaining weight. Regular consistent exercise, not binge exercise a few times a month.

The same is true when it comes to debt. Most people do not struggle with the weight of debt because of a single large purchase, like a house or car, which are intentional purchases, but from an accumulation of many small, less intentional or spur of the moment impulse purchases.

While our Rider may make some bad decisions and get us into trouble periodically, it's usually the Elephant who gets us into trouble with his intensity and impulsiveness. Hence, our challenge is motivating our elephant down a better and more sustainable path.

NOTES AND TAKE-AWAYS

INTENTIONALITY ELEMENTS TO IMPLEMENT

CHAPTER 16

TAKING OWNERSHIP AND AVOIDING FALSE HOPE

When a team takes ownership of its problems, the problem gets solved. It is true on the battlefield, it is true in business, and it is true in life.

— JOCKO WILLINK

From what I have heard and read about twelve-step programs—how organizations like AA (Alcoholics Anonymous) help alcoholics achieve and maintain sobriety—the first step is to acknowledge that you have a problem. The same is true when it comes to intentionality—we must be willing to admit that our trajectory won't get us to where we want to go, and we need to adjust our course. In addition, we must adopt a course of action that has the potential to get us where we want to go.

Intentionality requires us to own our current situation and adjust so that our trajectory is aligned with what we want to accomplish.

Changing direction requires taking ownership of our current situation. You need to acknowledge that your current 'plan' is not working and that you need a new plan, even if the new plan is just the old plan with some adjustments. Many people struggle to change course because they either authored their current plan or they bought into it. Either way, the current plan is comfortable and is based on a variety of habits—usually bad habits if the plan is not giving us a desired result.

It's hard for people to let go of something they have poured themselves into. Instead, it seems easier to keep hoping that, somehow, the current plan will start to produce better results. This is the definition of insanity: doing the same thing over and over and expecting different results.

It certainly is insanity to keep seeing negative results from a plan yet stick with that plan. Too often, we have invested a lot of effort into something, and it's hard to abandon that plan.

It's why many entrepreneurs lose not only their business, but their homes [used for collateral] as well. It's why many smokers keep smoking even after being warned by their doctors that doing so will lead to an earlier death. Gamblers who have a hard time stopping when they are winning, or even losing, are why casinos prosper. It's why almost everybody overeats and battles gaining weight. It's why we'd rather sleep than get up early to exercise. You get the idea.

The key to adopting a new and better plan is gaining awareness that the current plan is leading us in the wrong direction—to less of what we want [or failure].

Not only do you need awareness that your current actions are not producing desired results, but you need to own your current situation and commit to a cadence of actions that take you in a different direction.

This often requires us to experience some discomfort that leads to an epiphany. The discomfort can come from another person, who tells us we're fat, or a situation that reveals that our current plan is flawed, like having a heart attack or being diagnosed with type-two diabetes. In other words, we gain a new level of awareness—something happens that suggests our current course of actions is flawed relative to our ultimate desires.

In an earlier chapter, I introduced the Second Law of Thermodynamics, which states that all things are in a state of decline. Without intervention, all things get worse, decline, deteriorate, decay, etc. Acknowledging your current situation and owning your actions allows you to adopt a new plan and move in a new direction.

Until we acknowledge that our current trajectory is not taking us where we want to go, it will be hard for us to make necessary changes. A significant hurdle is accepting the fact that what we believe, our philosophy, is somehow flawed. Earlier, we talked about philosophy as representing what we really believe and the way you know what people really believe is by their actions. So, in order to go in a new and better direction, we need to adjust our philosophy. Then, we need to align our actions with our new philosophy.

A word of caution regarding hope as it relates to intentionality. Hope is a good thing, but false hope is dangerous.

Merriam-Webster defines hope as desire accompanied by expectation of or belief in fulfillment. Desire is a good thing and is one of the two biggest motivators in life—the other big motivator is fear. Hope without appropriate action that leads to positive outcomes is false hope. Remember, intentionality is purposeful action, where hope helps provide motivation.

In the next section, I will introduce the Intentionality Formula, a formula that anyone can adopt and apply to virtually any endeavor in order achieve the things they hope for.

NOTES AND TAKE-AWAYS

INTENTIONALITY ELEMENTS TO IMPLEMENT

SECTION THREE

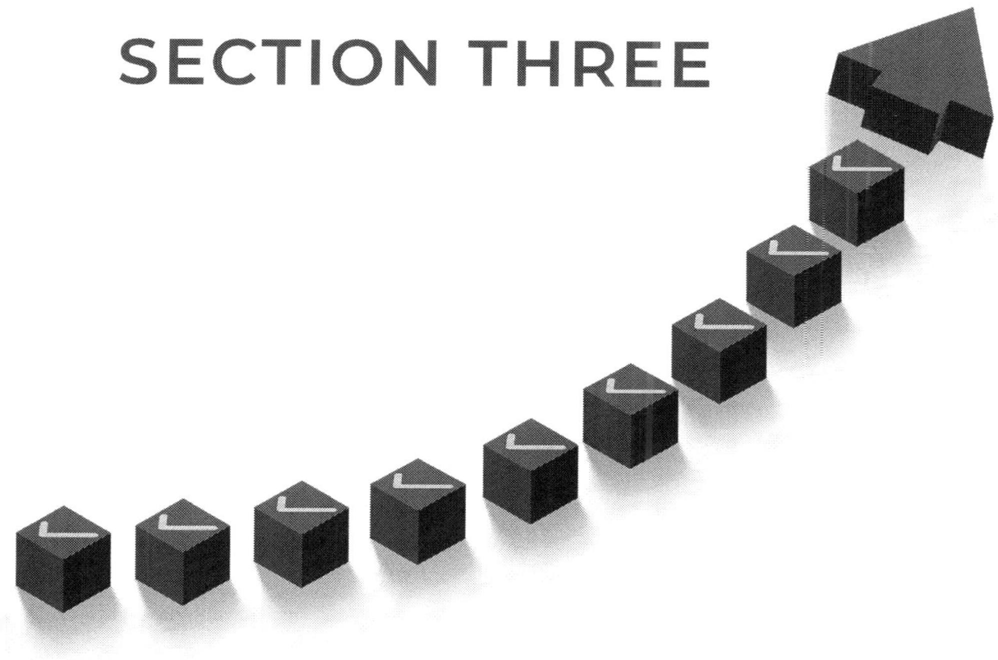

INTENTIONALITY FORMULA

CHAPTER 17

INTRODUCING THE FORMULA

Winning is not a sometime thing; it's an all the time thing. You don't win once in a while... you don't do things right once in a while... you do them right all the time. Winning is habit.

— VINCE LOMBARDI

Why do some teams win more than others? Why do some people achieve more of what they want than other people?

In the following section, I will introduce the Intentionality Formula and apply it to the efforts of teams. With minor tweaks, the Intentionality Formula can also be applied to the efforts of individuals in achieving more of what they want.

Whether it's a sports team, business team, or any other group of individuals, it seems that some teams win more than others. Why? What are the winning teams doing that the other teams aren't?

For the purpose of this section, let's agree that winning is defined as getting more of what you want, and losing is defined as getting less of what you want.

I'm convinced the ingredients for winning are available to anyone, but some people have a knack for putting the ingredients together in such a way that they can win more than others.

Just like how a cook combines readily available ingredients to make a tasty dish, I believe there are recipes and formulas that produce better outcomes than others. If you've ever tried cooking a recipe for the first time, you know what I mean.

The Intentionality Formula provides a framework for assessing virtually any situation to determine which aspects of our current effort are missing or need improvement.

In their book, *Extreme Ownership*, former Navy Seals Jocko Willink and Lief Babbin take lessons they learned in the military and adapt them to business.

After many tours of duty, Willink and Babbin retired and became Navy Seal Instructors. During one of their training sessions, they divided the thirty recruits into five teams of six and appointed one recruit in each group as the lead.

The teams competed in multiple grueling exercises, including one that required the teams to run along the beach and through the surf, carrying a rubber raft above their head.

Willink and Babbin observed that one team won every race, while another team lost most of the races. They came up with a theory for why this was happening and put it to the test. They swapped the leader from the winning team and the leader from the losing team and kept the rest of the teams the same.

As suspected, the team that had previously consistently won stopped winning, and the team that had previously consistently lost performed much better. Since they had not changed anything else, except for swapping leaders, Willink and Babbin concluded that there are no bad teams…only bad leaders.

So, what did the leader from the winning team do differently compared to the leader of the losing team? Well, not to be factious, but the winning leader did things differently than the losing leader. The winning leader better understood what needed to be done and executed a better formula, somewhat consciously and somewhat unconsciously or naturally.

I'm convinced that almost anyone can achieve better results by applying the Intentionality Formula to their endeavor.

The Intentionality Formula suggests that results are directly, and indirectly, correlated with four core components:

A. An Executable Plan
B. Engaged Talent
C. Commitment with Accountability
D. Feedback with Tweaks

These four components are divided into eight elements as represented in the following formula:

THE INTENTIONALITY FORMULA

Results are a direct function of the following inter-related elements:

A. 2 **Executable** 1 **Plan**

\+

B. 4 **Engaged** 3 **Talent**

\+

C. 5 **Commitment** & 6 **Accountability**

\+

D. 7 **Feedback** & 8 **Tweaks**

= X (RESULTS)

(© Mast 2023)

This suggests that, to practice intentionality, you simply follow eight simple steps:

1. Formulate a Plan
2. Ensure the Plan is Possible
3. Acquire the Quantity and Quality of Talent Necessary
4. Optimize Engagement
5. Gain Commitment [Buy-In] to the Plan
6. Provide Accountability, Not Policing

7. Seek and Embrace Feedback [Awareness]
8. Avoid Insanity by Making Appropriate Adjustments to the Plan

Let's unpack each of the elements individually in the next chapters.

NOTES AND TAKE-AWAYS

INTENTIONALITY ELEMENTS TO IMPLEMENT

CHAPTER 18

FORMULATE THE PLAN

PLAN: The first ingredient is always a plan—identifying what you want to accomplish, or where you want to end up, why you want to do it, and what steps will get you where you want to go. This is your THERE.

The Plan is all about clarity and coordination of action steps. People will stand around when they don't know what to do, or they will go off in multiple directions, typically their own direction rather than the intended direction, when they don't know or understand the team plan.

Stephen Covey, in his book *The Seven Habits of Highly Effective People*, called this beginning with the end in mind.

Lots of people have ideas, desires, and dreams but don't know how to get started and what steps to take. Most, if not all, people want more [of something]. Many hope they will get more of what they want but don't have a plan or action steps that will produce the kinds of results they ultimately want. So, remember that "hope is not a plan."

Brian Tracey, Canadian American motivational public speaker, and self-development author of more than eighty books including *The Psychology of Achievement*, said, "A goal without a plan is just a dream."

Sports teams have playbooks—plans that detail how each member of the team needs to execute plays, to move the ball down the field, and ultimately score points. Without a playbook, players are left running around in an uncoordinated manner, hoping to gain yards and score points.

So, the first step in the Intentionality Formula is to assess the quality of the plan. While no plan is perfect, to assess the quality of the plan, use a scale 0-10, where zero represents no plan and ten represents a perfect plan.

It's important that, in the initial assessment, you don't get caught up in too much detail and get stuck trying to get things exactly right—often referred to as paralysis by analysis.

Earlier in the book, we talked about gutfeel and that our emotional brains can give us direction even when we don't have all the answers. In the world of executive coaching, we often ask people who don't know an answer, "If you knew the answer, what do you feel it would be?" This is a way to back-door the brain and help a person get their rational brain out of the way and tap into their emotional brain. It's amazing how often people have a sense of what the answer might be but dismiss this gut feeling. So, the next time you're stuck, wondering what direction to take, tap into your gut feeling and take a step forward. You can always change directions if the initial step is not perfect.

Too many people hesitate to move forward toward their goals because they don't believe they have enough information to formulate a plan. As a result, they spend an inordinate amount of time researching when a little bit of gutfeel can get them started.

A business associate once shared a fascinating story that demonstrates this approach. It's titled *How Many Piano Tuners are there in Chicago?*

It was apparently the renowned physicist Enrico Fermi who came up with a type of estimation problem that is illustrated by the question, "How many piano tuners are there in Chicago?" Hence, it's known as a *Fermi Estimate*. The benefit of a Fermi Estimate is that it helps to measure a quantity that would otherwise be extremely difficult, if not impossible, to measure.

It gives people a way of thinking about a challenge in such a way as to come up with an answer or plan when they don't have the answers or insights, they think they need. The theory is that, deep down in our vast learning, we have enough information that we can string together enough reasonable estimates to come up with a sufficiently accurate answer and, in most situations, to allow us to keep moving forward in our analysis rather than getting stuck or delayed by over-analysis.

The premise is that numerons assumptions will often offset each other and provide a sufficiently accurate answer. Below is an example of how this plays out.

The process starts by asking, "How many piano tuners are there in Chicago?"

Faced with this question, most people will either answer, "I don't know," leaving them stuck, thinking they need to know the exact answer, or they start researching to see if they can find the right answer, delaying forward progress and wasting time. Certainly, getting answers to these kinds of questions is much easier with the Internet, but imagine the challenge everyone faced prior to the Internet. Still, why over-analyze a situation when you can cut through it in a fraction of the time?

This exercise is not ultimately about piano tuners as it is developing a thought process that helps avoid getting stuck in analysis and allows us to focus on what really matters.

For those that don't know what a piano tuner is (yes, there are many younger members of society that wouldn't know since so many things are digital now), it's a person who has a really good ear for sound and who utilizes their talent, skill, and tools to tune a piano so that each key makes the sound it's intended to make.

Full-size pianos have 88 keys, and each key is supposed to make the sound that relates to a standard note in the range of notes. Music is written using notes that specify certain sounds. If a pianist plays a piece of music on a piano that is out of tune, the resulting sound will be off and will not resemble the intended music.

Acoustic pianos make sound by a little hammer hitting a tightly drawn wire of varying thicknesses and tensions. Over time, and often each time a piano is moved, the wires either stretch or get looser, causing them to make a slightly different sound than their intended sound.

Tuning a piano involves a meticulous process of loosening or tightening the wires until the sound matches the sound of the appropriate tuning fork relating to that specific note. If you aren't familiar with what a tuning fork is, you can Google™ it.

Tuning is not required with digital pianos where the notes are digitally recreated.

Back to the story and the process of answering questions we don't believe we have enough information to answer.

Here is an example of the thought process regarding the number of piano tuners in Chicago:

1. First, ask yourself what the population of Chicago is. If you don't know, think about the city you live in. Do you know that population? If not, make a reasonable guess and then multiply or divide that number by how much bigger or smaller your city is compared to Chicago. If you live in Lincoln, Nebraska, for instance, you could guess that your city has a population of 230,000 and Chicago is maybe 20 times bigger. Whether 230,000 or 20 is exactly right is not as important as making several reasonable assumptions. Remember, the premise of this approach is that many reasonable assumptions have a way of balancing each other out, allowing us to arrive at a sufficiently accurate result to be able to take the next step in our decision process, rather than getting caught up in the paralysis of analysis. This is because low guesstimates will be offset by high guesstimates and vice versa. In this example, you would come up with a population for Chicago of 4.6 million people.
2. Next, estimate how many people there are in the average household. A household would generally only have one piano if they had a piano. I'm going to use the number of 2.5 people per household for this example. My thought process is that there are many single-person households and no-child households. To this point, the math suggests the number of households in Chicago is approximately 1.84 million.
3. Then estimate how many households would have a piano. I'm only counting acoustic pianos as electric pianos don't require tuning. I'm going to suggest that, in a sampling of 100 households, about 1/20 would have a piano. One out of twenty suggests that 5% have a piano, suggesting there are 92,000 acoustic pianos in Chicago.

4. Next is the question of how often the average piano needs tuning. I'm going to guess once every 5 years. Some people might do it more frequently; others might not ever get their piano tuned. This brings the number of pianos that need tuning each year to 18,400.
5. Now we need to ask how many pianos the average piano tuner can tune in a year. I'm thinking that a piano tuner might be able to do two to three a day. So, let's say 2.5 multiplied by 200 working days (being generous with vacation days) for a total of 500 pianos a year.
6. 18,400 divided by 500 suggests there are 37 piano tuners in Chicago.

If you do a Google search, you'll find that the number of Registered Piano Tuners (RTPs) in Chicago was 44 in 2009. So, this demonstrates that the Fermi approach produces a pretty good result.

This approach does not work for all situations, especially when precise answers are critical, but this approach certainly helps when you're stuck. And, once you get going with what really matters, you can gather more information and refine your plan.

So, the first step is to assess whether we feel our plan is a 3/10 or 8/10. This, then, together with the other elements of the Intentionality Formula will allow us to determine where to focus our efforts first.

NOTES AND TAKE-AWAYS

INTENTIONALITY ELEMENTS TO IMPLEMENT

CHAPTER 19

ENSURE THE PLAN IS POSSIBLE

EXECUTABLE: This refers to the plan being achievable or doable.

On the surface, this may seem like a silly element. Obviously, people wouldn't formulate plans that can't be achieved, right? You'd be surprised.

The issue here is not whether the plan can be undertaken, and the goal or objective achieved, but whether you or the team believe it can. Generally, people won't start and put effort into something unless they believe they can get where they want to go or achieve what they want to achieve.

Interestingly, a mistake that many managers make is to outline lofty goals with the hopes that the team will accomplish more than if they set lower, more achievable goals. Science doesn't support that approach. People need to believe the goal is achievable before they will put forward effort.

Research shows that people will be more motivated to undertake plans they believe are achievable and to push for greater achievements if they achieve them in a shorter period.

This was proven in my own life. I set out to lose 30 pounds in eight months. When I lost 30 pounds in five months, I kept going with my plan and was able to lose 50 pounds in eight months.

I'm convinced that people won't even try if they believe the goal isn't achievable.

Here's another example. Imagine if I suggested that I would pay you $1,000 for 4 hours of work? Most would jump at the opportunity until I told them that the four hours would be spent running without stopping.

Even though most marathon runners can run 26.2 miles within four hours, with the fastest time on record being 2:01:39, accomplished by the legendary Kenyan runner Eliud Kipchoge, you probably wouldn't take me up on my offer unless you are an avid runner already.

Leaders understand that people need to believe something is possible if they are to get buy-in from their team.

Many managers make the mistake of thinking that giving people [unrealistic] big goals will get them to try harder than giving them realistic goals. In reality the opposite is true. It's better to start with a realistic goal, set by the person who is to do the work, help them achieve the goal, and then help them push past the goal once they achieve it.

So, the second step is to assess how we feel about the execution of our plan on a scale of one to ten to determine the priority of this element.

NOTES AND TAKE-AWAYS

INTENTIONALITY ELEMENTS TO IMPLEMENT

CHAPTER 20

ACQUIRE THE QUANTITY AND QUALITY OF TALENT NECESSARY

TALENT: Even if there is a plan in place that we believe is executable, it's necessary to assess the quantity and quality of talent available.

Team members must have the talent and skills necessary for the endeavor. Jim Collins, author of *Good to Great*, refers to this as the right people on the bus and in the right seats.

There are many ways to gain insight into what talents are available. The simplest is to observe things that people are currently doing and enjoy doing. The two tend to go together.

Another way to gain insights into talents, or the things that come naturally to you, is to complete a talent or personality assessment as discussed above.

Never lose sight of the importance of effort. Here is a helpful formula:

TALENT + EFFORT = SKILLS
SKILLS + EFFORT = SUCCESS

While talents are those things that come naturally, skills are those things we are able to do with additional effort.

Even though effort can make up for a lack of talent, don't lose sight of the fact that, the more effort you need to put into something, the more difficult it will be to sustain it. This means that, while there are many things that you may be able to do, the things you have greater talent for will be much easier to do and more sustainable over time.

Michael Jordan was a great athlete. He had greater talent for basketball than baseball. He tried to play pro baseball and put in tremendous effort, but he could not compete compared to other more talented baseball players. In contrast, he became one of the greatest basketball players of all time because of his superior talent and incredible effort.

The third step, after considering the plan and its executability, is to assess how we feel about the quality of talent available. Again, use a scale of one to ten to assess this element of the formula and determine its priority.

NOTES AND TAKE-AWAYS

INTENTIONALITY ELEMENTS TO IMPLEMENT

CHAPTER 21

OPTIMIZE ENGAGEMENT

ENGAGED: Even when the quality of talent seems high, it's critical to assess the level of engagement.

Warm bodies are not enough. Those warm bodies need to be talented and want to do what we need them to do.

Measuring engagement has become big business, with organizations spending millions of dollars each year measuring and trying to increase team and individual engagement.

The Gallup Corporation has done extensive research into employee engagement, with some of the results shown in the graphic on the next page:

BENEFITS OF HIGH EMPLOYEE ENGAGEMENT

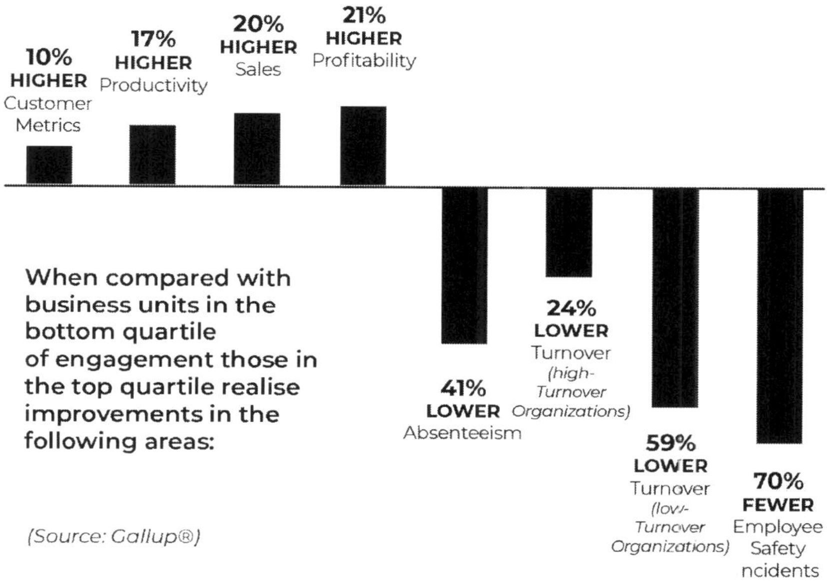

Studies show that highly engaged employees are twice as productive as unengaged employees. This explains why measuring engagement and improving the work environment can translate into a significant increase in an organization's bottom line.

Author Liz Wizeman, in her book *Multipliers*, provides insights into leadership behaviors that either increase or reduce team engagement. She calls leaders who create engaging environments multipliers and those who create unengaging environments diminishers because of the impact these environments have on a team.

So, just having talented people is not enough. Leaders must also be concerned with the environment they create to elevate engagement.

Since labor costs tend to be the biggest cost factor for organizations after the cost of goods, it's easy to see why investing in employee engagement can reduce the number of people required and/or boost production.

There are even investors who look for organizations with a good product but low employee engagement. They know they can significantly increase the value of the organization by simply increasing employee engagement.

It needs to be pointed out that, while increasing employee engagement may be simple, it's not easy and requires tremendous leadership.

The fourth step, then, is to assess how engaged we feel the talent is. As with the other elements, use a scale of one to ten to assess the level of engagement and to determine the priority of this element.

NOTES AND TAKE-AWAYS

INTENTIONALITY ELEMENTS TO IMPLEMENT

CHAPTER 22

GAIN COMMITMENT [BUY-IN] TO THE PLAN

COMMITMENT: One of my favorite statistics in football is yards after initial contact. I see this statistic as a fantastic measurement of commitment and desire. It's one thing to execute a play and achieve what was expected. It's a totally different level of commitment when a player fights for additional yards after they have been hit [or meet resistance]. And it's when the entire team possesses this level of commitment and desire that your odds of becoming a championship team increase.

Another word for commitment is buy-in. It's one thing to provide a team with clarity of expectations; that's important, but it's not enough. Leaders understand that people do much more of what they want to do than what they have to do. That's why they take time to gain buy-in and not only tell people what they expect from them.

Sure, it's more expedient to tell people what to do, but people who buy in will outperform those who do not.

The power is in the psychological ownership that buy-in provides. People who buy in will think about the task more, be more focused, remember to do it, and execute it with more desire.

Most leaders are Type-A, or dominant, personalities where telling others is more natural. Hence, it requires intentionality for most leaders to pause for the few additional minutes it takes to have a buy-in conversation.

Most buy-in conversations start with an explanation of why a particular task or project needs to be done. And it's in the alignment around the why that buy-in takes place. So, the next time you are tempted to tell people to do something, start with an explanation of why something needs to be done, and rather than telling them to do it, ask them if they would be willing to do it. Buy-in tends to take place in response to a question rather than a command.

The great thing about starting with *why* is that once a person understands the why they can usually figure out what needs to be done and how to do it to fulfill the why.

Here's a simple example contrasting two approaches. Jane and Ted are standing in the conference room. Jane is the Sales Manager, and Ted is one of the sales team members:

1. Telling Approach (Without Explaining the Why): Jane says, "Ted, please go get the ladder that is in the closet at the back of the warehouse." About 10 minutes pass, and then Ted reappears empty-handed and explains, "I looked in the closet, but there wasn't a ladder there."
2. Buy-in Approach (With an Explanation of Why): Jane turns to Ted and says, "This ceiling tile (pointing to the one in the corner of the conference room) has been hanging

> down for a few weeks now. I figure it's a simple fix. Ted, would you mind getting the ladder that's in the closet at the back of the warehouse?" About twelve minutes later, Ted comes back with a ladder and explains, "I looked in the closet, but there wasn't one there, so I looked around the shop until I found one."

When people are armed with why, they not only understand the importance of the request, but they have more information with which to make a choice as to whether they are going to comply with the request, and if they agree, they will go to greater lengths to fulfill the request.

As with the other elements, asses the level of commitment on a 0-10 scale to determine the priority of this element.

NOTES AND TAKE-AWAYS

INTENTIONALITY ELEMENTS TO IMPLEMENT

CHAPTER 23

PROVIDE ACCOUNTABILITY, STOP POLICING

ACCOUNTABILITY: Without commitment, or buy-in, it's not possible to provide true accountability. Most managers do what is called policing, rather than accountability.

Rather than telling people what to do, Leaders take time to explain the plan and why certain tasks are important. Then they ask the team, or team member, for their commitment. And to ensure commitment, they might even ask the person if they will be willing to be held accountable for the task.

Accountability means you are simply following up with the person on something they said they would do.

Most times however, managers follow up to ensure the person did what they were told to do, hence the expression, "Inspect what you expect," which is a form of policing.

A sure sign of policing is when a manager needs to repeatedly remind a team member to do something. This is also a form of micromanagement, which few people appreciate, or respond well to. Regardless, while policing may help produce short-term results, it doesn't produce longer-term and sustainable results.

Leaders ask and get buy-in. Managers tell and usually have to keep telling.

The key here is to get psychological ownership from the person who needs to complete the task. People who own things are more apt to remember, follow-through, and do a better job.

NOTES AND TAKE-AWAYS

INTENTIONALITY ELEMENTS TO IMPLEMENT

CHAPTER 24

SEEK AND EMBRACE FEEDBACK

FEEDBACK: Great leaders understand the importance of awareness, which I believe is a much better word than feedback.

Presumably, things are done for a reason, and awareness provides the feedback needed to potentially change course if the awareness suggests the current direction won't produce desired results.

Awareness comes from two sources: internal, or self-awareness, and external, or other-awareness. Another reason humility is such an important attribute for a leader is how it impacts how much external awareness a leader will avail themself of.

Arrogant leaders tend to rely too heavily on self-awareness, which is never sufficient.

That's why great leaders canvass their teams, their customers, their vendors, and their environments for as much awareness as possible to validate whether their trajectory is on target or not. Each one of these awareness sources is essentially a mirror.

Unfortunately, most people don't understand the true purpose of a mirror. When asked what they believe the true purpose of a mirror is, most people say something like, "to see yourself." But the true value and benefit of a mirror is so much greater.

To demonstrate and make my point, I often do an exercise with teams to help them understand and appreciate the true purpose and value of a mirror. I ask each person to hold their hands out in front of them and to look at their hands. Then I ask whether they can see their hands. Everybody readily acknowledges that they can see their hands [themselves] without a mirror. So, I ask what they need the mirror for. After some discussion, most groups ultimately arrive at the proper answer: to see things that we are otherwise not able to see.

That's the key to feedback, to gain awareness that we otherwise wouldn't have.

We started this section by talking about the importance of a plan and following a formula for driving better results. Measuring results and other key metrics, often referred to as KPIs (Key Performance Indicators), is a critical form of feedback that can come in the form of lagging or leading indicators.

Lagging indicators are those that provide awareness of what happened in the past—financial statements are one of the most popular forms of lagging indicators—what results have been achieved. Leading indicators, however, are those that provide awareness about the actions being taken to affect the results—daily activity logs would be an example of a leading indicator.

Results are the byproduct of actions. To get better results, track and improve the actions.

NOTES AND TAKE-AWAYS

INTENTIONALITY ELEMENTS TO IMPLEMENT

CHAPTER 25

AVOID INSANITY BY MAKING HELPFUL CHANGES

TWEAKS: Needless to say, without tweaks, we are doomed to repeat our past [and live a life of insanity]. Yet, it's surprising how often people gather feedback, with good intentions, and then don't act or change course. The reality is that knowing is not doing, and to get different results, something needs to change.

I have conducted many employee engagement surveys over the last decade, and one of the main reasons team members choose not to participate is that they don't believe anything is going to be done with the feedback they provide. This is often a fair sentiment as managers, while good at getting feedback, usually struggle to act on the feedback. It's not that they don't want to; it's that they are too busy doing what they have always done and don't take the time to implement change. Further, the longer we do what we have always done, the deeper the rut that we create.

I'm reminded of a story about the Alaska highway when it was still a dirt road. There was supposedly a sign at the beginning of the highway that read, "Choose your rut wisely because you will be in it for the next 500 miles."

Remember, while it's good to get feedback, it's equally, if not more, important to act on the feedback. Further, it's important that team members see change in response to their feedback. People need to feel that their voice made a difference if we want them to continue to give feedback.

Most people are happy to participate if they know the feedback is helpful and will be acted upon. Nobody wants to waste time and effort or be played as a fool. In terms of the Compassionate Candor Model, not acting on feedback is a form of Insincere Manipulation.

Most people have become cynical about surveys because organizations often just use them to check a box or use them as a scorecard and don't act on the feedback. In the retail world, many people don't give honest responses to customer surveys because they don't want somebody to get in trouble because of their response. On the flip side, they have become wise to the survey process and weaponize it to hold a seller hostage, either for a discount or additional benefits.

The Intentionality Formula provides a way for leaders, who are not happy with current results, to determine where they need to provide additional clarity or apply additional energy.

A leader can go through this process alone or have members of the team assess their situation. It's usually fascinating when members of the team assess the organization based on these eight elements independently and then compare notes. Doing so quickly reveals where a team is aligned and where it is disconnected. Then based on how each element is scored, the team has greater clarity of how to move forward.

NOTES AND TAKE-AWAYS

INTENTIONALITY ELEMENTS TO IMPLEMENT

SECTION FOUR

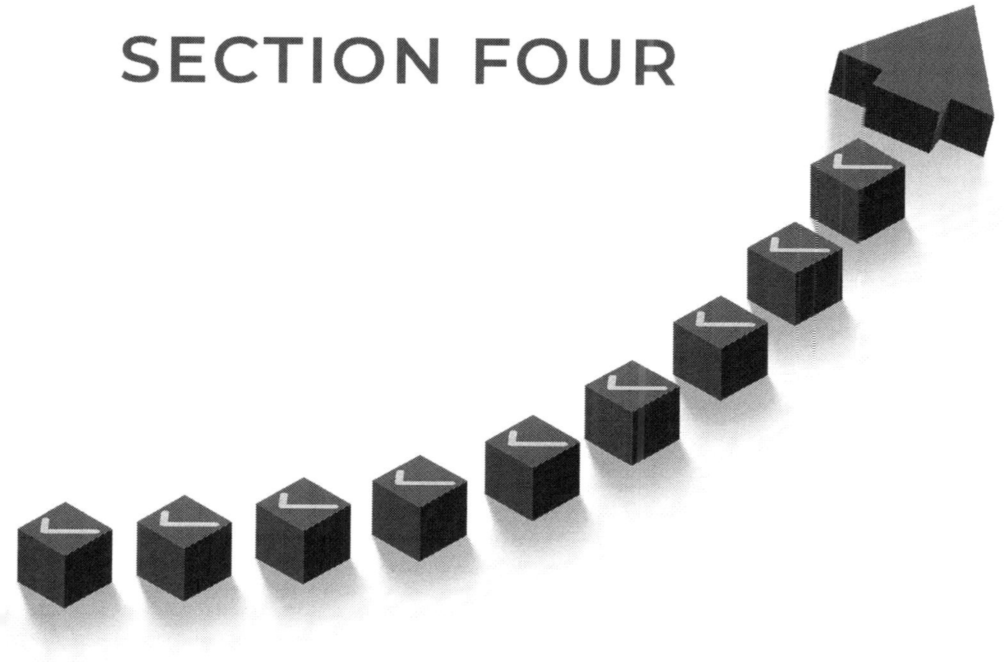

THE THREE INTENTIONALITIES OF A GREAT LEADER

CHAPTER 26

INTRODUCTION TO THE THREE INTENTIONALITIES

At the time of writing this book, I'm actively engaged in coaching leaders in the auto industry. As noted earlier in the book, this is not an industry that I chose, but rather one that seemed to choose me.

There are good reasons why the auto industry has gained the reputation it has. For many of those reasons, which are not relevant to expand on here, I never imagined working in this industry. I will also say that, on several occasions, I actively tried to go in a different direction, but I came to realize this is an industry where I feel I can make a difference, and isn't that what leadership is all about?

I should also point out that, with the amount of time I have spent in the auto industry, it's important for me to share two observations. First, the auto industry is not dissimilar to many, if not most, other industries, and there are many highly reputable dealers who get tarred because of the actions of the unethical few. The reality, however, is that since automobiles represent the second largest purchase most people will make in their lifetime and with the regular maintenance vehicles require, everybody's sensitivities are heightened when it comes to buying or servicing their vehicle.

Second, automobile dealerships are businesses with products and services offered and performed by people who need and benefit from greater leadership. The principles that guide any business or organization apply equally well to the auto industry.

Before I get into the details of the three Intentionalities of a great leader, let me tell you a brief story of how I entered the auto industry and how my future team felt about the prospect of somebody from the outside becoming their leader.

After a short stint working for a large Canadian Bank straight out of college, I spent many years as an entrepreneur until I focused heavily on the auto industry in 2009.

Many people, especially those within the auto industry, are surprised when I tell them that my very first role was that of General Manager. This is because the typical career path for a General Manager is to sell cars before being promoted to work in the finance department, then to manage a team of salespeople as one of the sales managers before getting the opportunity to be a General Manager. Few attain the level of General Manager, and the road to get there can take many years.

Maybe it also helped that, by nature, I'm a generalist. In college, I decided that I didn't want to focus on one area and took a wide range of courses. I was even pre-med but realized after my first year that I didn't want to go through medicine. So, after my first year, I switched to business. Then, as an entrepreneur, I was drawn to several different industries and gained a broad perspective of how business works.

Before taking the General Manager job, I had the opportunity to sit with each of the people that would be a part of my leadership team in the dealership. During one of those initial conversations with my General Sales Manager, who was the former General Manager of the store—you can already envision how that's going to go— he asks me straight up, "So, you've never been in the car business before? What are you going to bring [to the job and to the team]?"

Without hesitation, I asked him how many years he had been in the industry. He said twenty-five. I asked about the Parts Manager, and he said thirty-three. How about the Service Manager? He said thirty years.

I sense he was trying to make the case that, with all this experience, they knew what they were doing and didn't need an outsider to tell them how to run things—especially someone who did not have industry experience.

I responded, "So, what you're telling me is that we have in excess of 120 years of experience on the leadership team, and this is the level of performance you have to show for it." I continued, "I guess I'll bring the other stuff."

I know this might sound arrogant on the surface, but it wasn't. I'm not an arrogant person. It also wasn't intended to be cocky, but rather to make a point. The store's performance was not where the owners wanted it to be, and changes were necessary. So, the number of years of experience was just a diversion from the real issues that needed to be addressed.

I have found that anybody who uses years of service as validation or as a measure of competency tends to be closed to the real issues and not open to better solutions.

There is a reason some people, teams, and leaders achieve better results than others, and it tends to come down to recognizing and filling the gaps between what is being done and what needs to be done.

Every team has gaps. The biggest question is whether they are willing to acknowledge them.

Interestingly, the sentiment of filling gaps and connecting dots has largely defined my career, not only in the car business but as an entrepreneur and leadership coach.

In Section One, I provided insights into several gap-fillers, principles, and concepts that you may not have considered previously or may just have needed to be reminded of.

In Section Two, I introduced you to the Intentionality Model to provide a simple way of understanding that achievement is based on purposeful actions directed by what we really believe, our philosophy.

In Section Three, I shared with you the Intentionality Formula to help identify gaps and establish priorities for action.

In this Section, my objective is to give you a clear path for making your leadership more actionable and effective.

Everybody brings something to the table, but sometimes the element that will catch us unaware is what we don't know, and we often need an outsider to bring awareness to help fill those gaps.

I have gained tremendous encouragement from Alan Mulally's journey with Ford Motor Company. For many years, he was the CEO of Boeing Commercial Airplanes and then led Ford as CEO through some of its most challenging years.

While the other automotive CEOs snickered at the thought of Ford hiring a CEO who did not have previous automotive experience, Mulally contended that leadership is about consistently applying principles to the operation of a business, principles that transcend industries. He proved this to be correct through his eight years with Ford. For that, he earned the acknowledgement as one of the greatest CEOs of all time.

His story is chronicled by Bryce G. Hoffman in his book, *American Icon: Alan Mulally and the Fight to Save Ford Motor Company.*

Our gaps, the things we are missing, can represent a serious challenge. Hence, the first intentionality of a great leader involves assembling the right team. The second intentionality involves creating the right environment, and the third involves developing people to be their best. These three Intentionalities need to define your leadership if your team is to achieve extraordinary results and optimal performance.

NOTES AND TAKE-AWAYS

INTENTIONALITY ELEMENTS TO IMPLEMENT

CHAPTER 27

INTENTIONALITY #1

ASSEMBLE AND SHAPE A HIGH PERFORMANCE TEAM

Remember from earlier, intentionality means you're doing things on purpose and with a purpose. It's not about random action and not just about having good ideas or intentions, nor talking about what you're going to do, or engaging in actionless goal setting. Intentionality is all about taking purposeful action in alignment with your overriding philosophy.

Sometimes, you get the opportunity to hire people and assemble a team. Other times, you inherit an existing team. Both have their own set of challenges. Regardless, as Jim Collins, author of *Good to Great*, stresses, you need to get the right people on the bus.

When you get to hire new people, it's important you hire the right people. If you want to build a high-performance team, you need to hire high-performance team members. I know that sounds obvious, but most hiring managers struggle with hiring the right people. It's not something that comes naturally to most people. Other times, they lack the training and time to make better hires. That's why so many managers hire warm bodies to fill empty seats on the bus. Unfortunately, warm bodies rarely work in the long term leads to high turnover and result in higher hiring and training costs.

A brief point here about the intentionality with which you assessable or shape a team. Leaders need to understand that the higher you are in an organization, the less direct impact you will have on the results the organization produces. This is often a difficult concept for managers to grasp.

While you will have an impact on the results the organization produces, the impact will be indirect. Indirect, as the results will be produced by the team that you either bring on board or allow to stay. Your team produces the results with your direction and encouragement.

Simon Sinek, author of *Leaders Eat Last*, suggests that team members are the ones who produce results and that a leader's focus needs to shift from producing results to caring for the people who produce the results. Further, think about how particular you are about the people you invite into your home and those you go on vacation with. You should be at least as intentional about the people you hire.

More times than not, leaders inherit an existing team and need to figure out who fits and who doesn't. In these situations, the focus needs to be on shaping those who fit into the high-performance team you desire.

It's great if you have objective metrics upon which to assess a person. Unfortunately, metrics are not always readily available.

Not to worry, you still have another powerful assessment tool available—your emotional brain from which comes your gutfeel. Remember from Section One that the emotional brain doesn't have the capacity to speak, but it has an incredible ability to gather and process unspoken information.

Certainly, gather all the metrics you can, but understand that metrics represent rational data. Since most hiring decisions are made based on how you feel about an individual, it's important that you tap into your emotional brain to help you make better hiring decisions. As discussed above, you do this by asking yourself emotionally structured questions about how you feel about the person on a scale of 1 to 10 on each of the elements detailed below. It's like taking inventory, which is something we will also use later in this section when it comes to assessing existing team members as part of establishing a coaching relationship.

But for now, we need to focus on the three key elements from which to assess team members: Capability, Cohesion, and Hunger.

Capability: First Key to Assessing Team Members

It seems like a no-brainer to say you need to hire or have capable people on your team. Surprisingly, many leaders don't know how to assess capability properly. Resumes don't always have metrics, and if they do, the metrics are often embellished. Further, just because somebody sat in a chair or behind a desk for a period, doesn't mean they possess proficiency.

You can also call references. Hopefully, the references are objective and are not friends with the prospect. In our current litigious society, it's also increasingly challenging for references to speak freely, fearing they might say something that could be used against them.

A conversation with somebody who worked with the prospect can be helpful, although surprisingly, many hiring managers don't always follow through and call. If and when they do call, they don't know what to ask to get helpful information.

So, to practice intentionality regarding assessing capability, it's important to look at two aspects of capability: Ability/Talent and Capacity/Potential.

- **Ability/Talent:** There are people who have talent, but for some reason have limited capacity or potential. So, you want to measure both.

  Ability or talent is the raw material you're born with. People have lesser or greater levels of abilities and talents. Think of Michael Jordan. He had a talent for both basketball and baseball. Sometimes, it's hard to measure the exact level of raw talent, but as we develop our talents, our level of potential or capacity becomes more obvious. In Michael Jordan's case, the more he worked at both sports, the more it became obvious that he had greater potential in basketball.

  An analogy that might help make the point is to consider a gold mine. Talent is analogous to the fact that gold is present. Capacity or potential speaks to the amount of gold present.

  Assessing talent and potential can be hard, but this is where our gut can help us. It's amazing how we can talk to somebody, and while our rational brain tries to sort out the words, our gut [emotional brain] develops a sense of how we might rate them on a scale of 1-10 on any given topic, especially when we develop the skill of asking better questions.

Asking somebody about the things they did in their youth will give insights into their level of talent. Asking them what they did in later stages of life and how proficient they felt, what awards they achieved, how active they are in the same areas gives insight into their capacity or potential.

DiSC™ assessments provide insights into what characteristics come naturally. For instance, salespeople tend to be enthusiastic, active, collaborative, outgoing, and relationship focused. While accountants tend to be reserved, task-oriented, organized, stable, and focused on accuracy. Matching the person's personality with the job will allow them to do the job with less energy and for longer periods of time.

- **Capacity/Potential:** Oftentimes, people may push back on their personality assessment, especially if it's the first time they have undergone such an exercise because they interpret the assessment as telling them they are less capable to do certain things. Most of us can do just about anything we want. The question is just whether that activity energizes or drains. Activities that drain are difficult to sustain for longer periods of time and will take a greater level of intentionality. They are draining because intentionality takes effort.

A salesperson can certainly be organized and detail-oriented if they really work at it, but they are not known for that in the manner an accountant would be. In a similar manner, accountants could do sales but choose not to because they find greater joy and accomplishment in work behind the scenes.

In this way, a personality assessment gives insights into our capacity or potential to do things. It's a great tool that can provide deep insights.

With capacity and potential assessments, like with the other elements in the first intentionality, using a scale of 1-10 can be extremely useful to cut through the lack of exact metrics.

The goal is to gain insights into whether the person has the necessary level of capability relative to the expectations and demands of the job. Poor hires are often the result when we don't assess candidates correctly.

Cohesiveness: Second Key to Assessing Team Members

The old game of tug-of-war is a quick example of the importance of cohesiveness in teams.

I worked with a client in Davenport, IA for many years, and they told me about their annual tug-of-war contest with a town on the other side of the Mississippi River in Illinois. The two didn't get together in the same city. They literally had a rope long enough to span the width of the river. Their teams would be on their respective side of the Mississippi, and upon notice to pull, each team would try to pull the other into the river.

Tug-of-war demonstrates that capability [strength] is not enough, as it might be in arm wrestling or other solo endeavors. It's important that members of a tug-of-war team are well coordinated [cohesive] in their efforts, pulling in the same direction at the same time.

Patrick Lencioni, in his book *The Advantage: How Organizational Health Trumps Everything Else in Business*, presents a model for understanding the idea of organizational health. His premise is that being smart [capable] is not enough to succeed as a team. He suggests that smart people are easy to find, but people who work well together are not.

The Organizational Health Model suggests that four elements are required:

1. A Cohesive Team
2. Organizational Clarity
3. Over-communication of Organizational Clarity
4. Embedding Organizational Clarity into Every Facet of the Organization in Order to Reinforce It.

Within the first quadrant, he shows how a cohesive team is the result of five elements:

- A foundation of vulnerability-based trust
- Open, candid discussion of issues (healthy conflict)
- Commitment
- Accountability
- A focus on common and shared goals

So, to practice intentionality regarding assessing capability, it's important to look at two aspects of capability: Alignment and Trust.

- **Alignment:** One of the best tools available to assess alignment is the vision, mission, and value statements of the organization. These documents are meant to be more than just a check-the-box exercise, wallpaper for the conference room, and marketing statements. These statements are meant to provide insights into what's important to the organization so the prospective or existing team member can decide if that is the cart they are willing to pull forward.

Above, I presented the cart analogy and suggested the cart represents the vision, mission, and values of the organization. Existing and prospective team members need to constantly evaluate whether they want to be tethered or yoked to this kind of cart. This is the *Why* that Simon Sinek refers to in his book *Start with Why*.

It's important that the Why of the organization is well matched to the Why of the team member. Why is also something that is processed by the emotional brain, which suggests that aligned individuals will share the purpose of the organization and will be that much more engaged in their work as a result.

Years ago, I was speaking with an organization about me joining them as one of their consultants. One of the first things they did was provide me with a single-page outline of their vision, mission, values, and guiding principles and asked me whether I was uncomfortable with any of the items listed there. I thought this was an awesome exercise. Better to know up front than to bring a person on board that is misaligned.

Here again, using a scale of 1-10 can be very helpful. I often suggest that managers provide prospective candidates with a list of the organization's vision, mission, values, and guiding principles and ask them to rate their alignment with each of the items.

Not only does this exercise open up many areas for further discussion, allowing the emotional brain to formulate its gutfeel, but it also provides a simple way to see how aligned the candidate is with what's important to the organization.

- **Trust:** Here we are concerned with whether the person is willing to be vulnerable.

  In the Organizational Health Model above, vulnerability-based trust is the foundation of a healthy and functional organization. Vulnerability is important because it's at the heart of authenticity. We want to be able to take people at face value and not be left wondering and second-guessing what they say, or whether they are wearing a work mask.

  Vulnerable people are willing to admit when they are wrong or need help. They are able to apologize and admit when others are better than them at something. It's not hard to see why, in this sense, vulnerability is not only a strength but desirable. You might recall from the discussion of the DiSC™ assessment that we all have things we are good at and not so good at. Things that come naturally and things that don't. When interviewing people, you will sense their authenticity, and you will naturally build greater trust with people who are willing to admit to things they are not good at or don't enjoy.

When you ask appropriate questions, it won't be hard for your emotional brain to give you a gutfeel for what number they rate 1-10.

Hunger: Third Key to Assessing Team Members

This should be an easy concept to grasp. In the same way that hungry people will eat more, hungry people from a work perspective will produce more. Sadly, work ethic is not always something you can teach.

I believe work ethic can be instilled over time and nurtured, but hunger is something that is more closely tied to alignment around a sense of purpose. Hunger is about desire, passion, and effort.

- **Desire:** I'll never forget when and where I was when this concept made sense to me. I was attending summer camp at age nine, and our counselor gathered us around and talked to us about motivators. He said that ultimately in life there are two motivators: fear and desire. Some people are more motivated by fear, and others are more motivated by desire.

  Fifty years later, I had a coaching conversation with a General Manager. He shared that he believes people are either more motivated by the fear of failing or the desire to win. He admitted to me that he is more motivated by the fear of failure.

  After giving it some thought, I suggested that I'm much more motivated by the desire to achieve and win. I'm sure a big part of that is a result of my personality, which comes out in two specific ways: First, I have a high propensity for risk, which served me well when I was an entrepreneur. Second, according to the Gallup® StrengthsFinder assessment, Achiever is my highest talent trait. So, not only am I not afraid to lose, but I need to achieve. My sense of fulfillment is boosted when I get stuff done and takes a hit when I don't accomplish something significant each day.

Again, try to rate people's level of desire on a scale of 1-10. Asking questions about what they like to do in their free time will help. If an auto technician talks about the modifications they have made to their own vehicle in the evenings and on weekends, it will suggest a high level of desire.

- **Passion:** Passion is closely tied to desire. I'm reminded of an automobile salesperson I heard about in Las Vegas who got the nickname Mustang Manny. Manny was his first name, and he loved Ford Mustangs so much that he not only owned one but modified it extensively. I never saw his car but heard many stories. His desire was so high for Mustangs that he didn't want to sell anything else. The dealership recognized this and built him his own website to be able to promote and sell Mustangs. It's amazing how people are motivated when they feel a sense of passion. It's also amazing how people connect with others who share similar passions.

What level of passion do you sense from the team member on a scale of 1-10?

- **Effort:** What some people lack in talent they make up through effort. Effort is universally valued. Effort is not just physical but can be mental as well.

  Assessing effort is helpful when adding new team members.

  One of my favorite statistics in football is yards after initial contact. This is a sign of both desire and effort. Some will feel they have accomplished the task when they run their route and will lie down as soon as they are hit. Others will keep driving even if it's for a few additional inches. Often those inches result in additional feet and/or yards. This is the essence of intentionality, doing the little things that seem as easy to do as not to do.

  You might recall the formula presented earlier which emphasize the importance of effort:

  TALENT + EFFORT = SKILLS
  SKILLS + EFFORT = SUCCESS

What level of effort do you sense the team member typically gives on a scale of 1-10?

NOTES AND TAKE-AWAYS

INTENTIONALITY ELEMENTS TO IMPLEMENT

CHAPTER 28

INTENTIONALITY #2

CREATE AND MAINTAIN AN ENGAGING ENVIRONMENT

When talking about the importance of good environments, the analogy of a farmer is helpful.

I'll start with a humorous example. It's a story about a city guy who heard there was great money in raising chickens. So, he bought himself a piece of land in the country and started a chicken farm. To get the farm going, he went to the chicken wholesaler and bought 5,000 baby chicks. The wholesaler was pleased to have a new customer and happily assisted him with his purchase and wished him well.

A few weeks passed when the farmer came back to the wholesaler to purchase another 5,000 baby chicks. The wholesaler gladly obliged and was quietly surprised at the success that this new farmer was obviously having.

Another few weeks passed, and the farmer came back to the wholesaler to purchase another 5,000 baby chicks. This time, the wholesaler couldn't contain his curiosity and asked what the secret to his success was. The farmer looked down and admitted that things were not going so well as the baby chicks kept dying. Embarrassed, he admitted that he wasn't sure if he was planting them too deep or too far apart.

Seriously…farming can provide us with excellent insights into what it means to practice intentionality regarding growing conditions.

The farmer understands that the environment, including moisture, sunshine, soil conditions, heat, etc. has a huge impact on the kind of harvest they can expect to get. Certainly, there are many positive and negative factors beyond the farmer's direct control (temperature, sunshine, rain, excessive winds, hail, etc.), but they also know there are many things within their control (aeration, nutrients, watering, tilling, etc.). They also know that whatever they do needs to be done early in the growing cycle and consistently. They trust that what they do will impact the ultimate crop.

Interestingly, I have found that many managers and business owners neglect their soil conditions and then wonder why the crop is not as bountiful as hoped for. It's almost as though they believe they can force the seed to grow.

Creating and maintaining an engaging environment with intentionality involves these three elements: Safety, Support, and Positivity.

Safety:

This is not just about physical safety but includes emotional, mental, and psychological safety.

Physical safety can be obvious and has been addressed by legislation and many regulations over the years. OSCA and Workers Compensation are the two most obvious. It's unfortunate when managers and owners are more concerned with boosting the bottom line at the expense of their people, such that an environment needs to be legislated.

Physical safety is not a zero-sum game, meaning that we only get a dollar of production for every dollar spent on safety. Rather, since a lack of safety can be a distraction, I believe a lack of safety ultimately costs the owner much more than the savings retained. Further, whether an owner creates a safe environment or not sends a message of how much they value their people.

Under the Intentionality Formula, I shared that the average American worker is only 48% engaged. Discretionary [want to] effort averages 30-60%. In other words, team members choose whether they are going to contribute at a higher or lower level depending on how they feel.

This suggests that attention to the work environment of an organization can have a significant return on investment. This is not just the actual safety of the environment, but also the perceived safety.

One of my automobile clients had a tragic accident in their repair shop—a technician was crushed under a vehicle when the lift seemed to fail. After a thorough investigation, it was determined the accident was due to human error. Regardless, understanding how important both actual and perceived safety is, the dealership had that lift and all other lifts in the shop safety inspected and recertified to eliminate any perception of unsafe lifts. This minimized the fear and distraction of technicians and allowed them to focus on their work.

Ensuring that a workplace honors the dignity of all team members is important to minimizing psychological safety elements. Dignity involves the things that people cannot control, like their race, age, gender, height, etc. When team members make fun of others because of one or more of these inherent elements, it's not only uncomfortable but unsafe for all involved.

Honoring dignity builds safety and allows love, loyalty, and free exchange between team members. Dishonoring dignity leads to anger, conflict, and the desire for revenge.

Things like bullying defy emotional safety and should not be allowed.

Support:

Imagine a weightlifter going for their personal best or pushing for extra reps. What does the trainer do? He/she spots them. When the trainer or a friend is there to spot, the athlete will feel more comfortable to push further than they may have gone previously.

The same would be true for a gymnast, or many other athletes, who attempt to do things they had not done previously. Having sufficient support available gives the athlete additional confidence, knowing there is a safety net in case they can't quite do it.

A lack of confidence is a tremendous distraction for team members in organizations as well. Managers need to realize that a big part of building a high-performance team involves having time available to support team members when they need it.

Later, I'm going to emphasize the importance of doing regular one-on-ones with team members. I believe group meetings are for informing and encouraging, but correction and development happen one-on-one.

It's during those one-on-ones that a team member can share areas where they need additional support. Sadly, most managers are too busy and abdicate their responsibility in this area and consequently don't support their team members adequately.

Positivity:

According to Dr. Barbara Fredrickson, positivity researcher at the University of North Carolina, high-performance teams are three times more positive than negative.

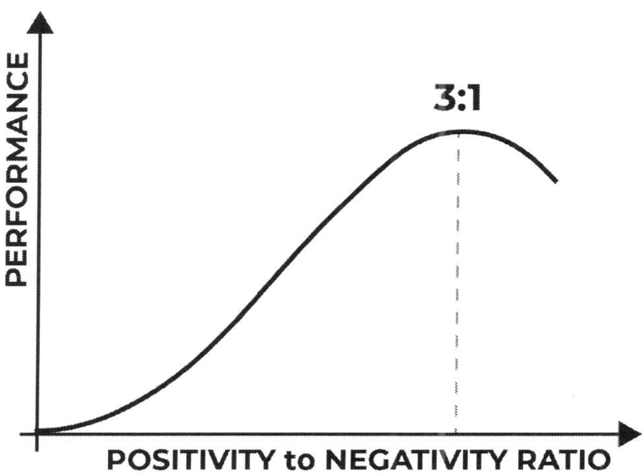

"Positivity doesn't mean we should follow the axioms Grin and bear it or Don't worry, be happy," Fredrickson says. "Those are simply superficial wishes. Positivity runs deeper. It consists of the whole range of positive emotions—from appreciation to love, from amusement to joy, from hope to gratitude, and then some."

Is high performance the result of positivity, or is positivity a by-product of high performance? It doesn't matter. The point is that higher positivity provides for an environment that's more conducive to performance. The caveat is that beyond 3:1 positivity loses its authenticity and loses its impact.

So, the goal for leaders is to create as positive an environment as possible while keeping it real. Keeping it real means not shying away from the difficult and uncomfortable conversations that give people the feedback they need to adjust their behaviors toward better performance. Such feedback can be viewed as critical and negative, so it needs to be offset with high degrees of positivity.

Some use the technique of a feedback sandwich whenever they need to give somebody feedback. The feedback sandwich suggests that, whenever you need to provide feedback, you start with positivity, then provide the negative feedback, and end with more positivity. While this may work for some, my concern is in using this technique with authenticity. As soon as it's perceived as a technique, it loses all its positive impact.

Negativity triggers cortisol, the hormone that shuts down the emotional brain and puts people into a reactionary fight, flight, or freeze mindset.

Positivity, on the other hand, allows the release of chemicals that stimulate the emotional brain, which in turn creates an internal [mental] environment that fosters collaboration, creativity, innovation, and relational connections.

D DOPAMINE
O OXYTOCIN
S SEROTONIN
E ENDORPHIN

The key to positivity with intentionality is being as positive as possible while providing compassionate candor (deep care with direct challenge).

A couple simple approaches to increase the positivity to negativity ratio are as follows:

- Minimize every kind of negativity that is not constructive.
- Increase the amount of authentic praise and recognition given to team members. Start with managers being more intentional with their praise and recognition and help that mindset take root as part of your culture. One way to do this is to use the three-penny approach: Put three intentionality pennies in your right pocket at the start of the day. Each time you praise or recognize somebody during the day, move one of the pennies to your left pocket. If at any time you say or do anything negative, move all pennies back to your right pocket. The goal is to end the day with all three pennies in your left pocket. Some people are natural encouragers; others may need a little help. The three-penny approach will add intentionality.

To order your own Intentionality Pennies, click on this QR Code. They are inexpensive and will help you increase positivity.

NOTES AND TAKE-AWAYS

INTENTIONALITY ELEMENTS TO IMPLEMENT

CHAPTER 29

INTENTIONALITY #3

COACH TEAM MEMBERS TO BE THEIR BEST

If you are being intentional about assembling and shaping a high-performance team and if you are intentionally working on creating, and are maintaining, an engaging environment, then the remaining element is to intentionally coach team members to be their best.

Everybody brings something slightly different to the table, and everybody has a different level of performance that would represent their best. It's incumbent upon the leader to help each person get to and operate at their best, not only for the benefit of the organization, but for the health and well-being of the individual.

I'm convinced that none of us feels true fulfillment when we are not operating at our best. I believe we all have an innate need to contribute, and we don't feel good when we are underperforming our best.

There's an interesting passage of scripture that reinforces this mindset. The following is from Matthew 25: 14-27 (Message translation):

> [14-18] "It's also like a man going off on an extended trip. He called his servants together and delegated responsibilities. To one he gave five thousand dollars, to another two thousand, to a third one thousand, depending on their abilities. Then he left. Right off, the first servant went to work and doubled his master's investment. The second did the same. But the man with the single thousand dug a hole and carefully buried his master's money.
>
> [19-21] "After a long absence, the master of those three servants came back and settled up with them. The one given five thousand dollars showed him how he had doubled his investment. His master commended him: 'Good work! You did your job well. From now on, be my partner.'
>
> [22-23] "The servant with the two thousand showed how he also had doubled his master's investment. His master commended him: 'Good work! You did your job well. From now on, be my partner.'
>
> [24-25] "The servant given one thousand said, 'Master, I know you have high standards and hate careless ways, that you demand the best and make no allowances for error. I was afraid I might disappoint you, so I found a good hiding

> place and secured your money. Here it is, safe and sound down to the last cent.'
>
> 26-27 "The master was furious. 'That's a terrible way to live! It's criminal to live cautiously like that! If you knew I was after the best, why did you do less than the least? The least you could have done would have been to invest the sum with the bankers, where at least I would have gotten a little interest."

The point is that we all have some degree of talent, and as such, we all have the responsibility to do our best with what we have. To do less than our best is a waste of our talents.

Sadly, this scenario plays out in organizations around the world every day. In one of my coaching sessions, a Sales Manager asked me what he should do with a salesperson who is not producing. He shared that some months the person achieves acceptable sales numbers, but generally, they are not. I asked him about his 1:1 cadence, and he admitted that they had not been intentional in doing 1:1s with their people. I then asked how long this person had been with the organization, and he said fifteen months.

Implementing Intentionality #3 will allow a sales manager to determine whether a person is the right fit for the organization and role within 60 to 90 days and certainly within the typical probationary period that most organizations have.

It's a travesty, both for the organization and the individual, and pure neglect to allow team members to go fifteen months without proper support and development, which is what Intentionality #3 is ultimately about. So, why is this so prevalent? Because our managers are not taught how to practice intentionality, and the leaders above them don't practice it themselves. What a waste of talent, time, and resources!

We should not feel bad about parting company with people who don't fit the organizational culture and/or are not able to perform at appropriate levels. We should feel bad when we hold people back from opportunities that are better suited for them elsewhere. The goal of keeping people on the team should be win/win. When it stops being a win for the organization, it also stops being a win for the individual and vice versa.

I encourage leaders to look at it from four perspectives:

1. **Impact on the rest of the team:** When you allow somebody to stay on the team when they are either not performing or they are affecting the team in some other way, you are essentially subsidizing the poor performer at the cost of the rest of the team. In other words, you are taking something away from the rest of the team when you tolerate contrary behaviors.
2. **Loss of leadership capital:** Most leaders don't realize how their personal stock goes down when they tolerate contrary behavior, but it's like what happens when a company doesn't perform to investors' expectations and the stock's value diminishes on the exchange. Leaders who operate with conviction, clarity, consistency, and commitment to organizational values gain value in the eyes of their team members. This value is what's called leadership capital, and it translates into authority with team members. Leaders who have leadership capital have greater authority with team members. Leaders who lack leadership capital must rely on power to get things done.

3. **Ultimate impact on the individual:** Anything that is not win/win is lose/lose and lose/lose is not sustainable in any relationship. Hence, if you feel like continuing to have a certain person on your team represents a loss situation for you, it suggests that it's also a loss for the other individual. This means that it's incumbent upon the leader to have a difficult conversation with the individual, determine if course corrections are possible, and if not, move in different directions for the benefit of both parties. Not everybody will immediately see the win in parting company, but there are many stories about people who were encouraged to leave a company and later came back and thanked the leader for parting ways with them. Had the leader not made the move, the other person would have persisted longer in a no-win situation. Instead, they were forced out of the nest and learned how to fly.
4. **Opportunity cost:** Every time you commit to one thing, you do so at the cost of being able to do something else. The more you tolerate something that is not working, the higher the cost of that choice compared to other available alternatives. Think of it in terms of investment. If you have $1,000 and you decide to invest it in ABC Company, that $1,000 is no longer available to invest in XYZ Company. In the same way, the longer you tolerate a contrary individual, the higher the cost associated with what could be. Very rarely do I hear from leaders and team members that they wished the organization had waited longer to deal with contrary situations. Normally, you will hear people say, *"What took you so long!"*

Coaching team members to be their best with intentionality is a way to ensure the employment arrangement is a win for both parties. Coaching teams requires leaders to invest in desire and practice intentionality.

Investing in Desire:

Remember the expression, "You can lead a horse to water, but you can't make it drink." I've come to learn there is tremendous truth to this statement.

There is also another ancient expression that says, "Don't give your pearls to swine." This is fairly harsh on the surface, but essentially suggests you shouldn't give your best to people who don't appreciate what you are giving them.

You can't make people do anything they don't want to do, and in the process of trying, you will wear yourself out and lose a sense of your own self-worth. It's energizing, joyful, and fulfilling to invest in people who appreciate your investment, but it's draining, frustrating, and discouraging trying to help somebody who doesn't want help.

They may not always say they don't want help, but their actions give them away. I was doing 1:1s with the team members of one of my clients. The 1:1 sessions were voluntary and offered to managers. They could go online and choose a time that worked best for them during the days I was on-site. I was surprised when one of the managers came to the conference room for his 1:1 and I shared that sentiment with him, to which he replied, "Herb, the optics are not lost on me." In other words, he knew the leaders of the organization were observing who was participating in the 1:1s and who wasn't. So, he felt political pressure to participate. The 1:1 was somewhat strained, and I doubt he took anything from it.

So, the first step in coaching team members to be their best is to determine if they have the desire to be coached.

1. **Take Inventory of Potential/Performance:** Above, we talked about assembling and shaping a high-performance team. I presented an approach where you rate the capability, cohesion, and hunger of team members on a scale of 1-10.

   The numbers you came up with were a form of inventory-taking. For each person, you will end up with an evaluation, which is your assessment of what they bring to the organization based on the six elements.

   Next, determine their level of agreement with the numbers you came up with in your evaluation.

2. **Self-Perception:** It's important that you write down your numbers so that you can have a candid conversation with the individual you are coaching.

   You start the conversation by telling the team member that you have rated them based on your gutfeel of things they have shared with you and things you have observed in them. You share with them that, because you care about them and their development, you will share openly and candidly what answers you have written down. First, however, you tell them that you would like to hear how they rate themselves.

   The goal here is four-fold. First, you want to assess how aligned the two of you are in your answers. Then you need to have substantive conversations around significant differences in your ratings. Next, you must determine their fit (if it's a prospective team member) or where there are areas of opportunity (if it's an existing team member). Finally, you determine how best to move forward.

This conversation is a form of calibration, and it's very difficult to move forward without alignment. Think of the GPS in your vehicle. How helpful are the directions if your GPS thinks your vehicle location is somewhere else, even if it's just 100 feet away from where the satellite thinks the road is. This has happened to me in construction zones where I'm detoured on temporary roads. It makes the GPS go squirrely as it tries to get you back on route, because the location of your vehicle just won't match what the GPS says are the available roads.

Further, if people believe they don't need help, it's a fool's errand to try to help them. If, however, they recognize where they need help, the two of you can journey together without unnecessary frustration and conflict.

The goal here is to determine whether you are aligned and whether there is enough untapped potential available to move forward. You can develop an underperforming person with talent if they recognize the need for help, but there's no point in investing in them if their best is not sufficient to get the job done.

Imagine interviewing a placekicker for your football team. They talk about their past experience kicking field goals, and it sounds like they have talent, but their best kick to date was only 25 yards. That may be fine for junior teams but far from sufficient for college teams, let alone a pro team. So, unless you both believe they have the potential to make much longer field goals, why would you consider them for your team?

3. **Coachability:** Aligning around the six elements is the important first step. The second step is identifying where the opportunities for development exist. Third, determine their level of coachability.

   To determine their level of coachability, you ask the team member two important questions: Do you want to achieve more of your potential? Do you want my help?

   If they don't want to improve and/or want your assistance, you have nothing to work with. It's time to have a different conversation.

   On the other hand, at the moment they agree they want to achieve more of their potential and they want your assistance, you have become their coach. Now you can move forward and put a plan in place with intentionality.

Practice Intentionality:

Having the foregoing conversation is necessary to determine where the opportunities exist and whether there is sufficient alignment and desire to move forward, but it's not enough. Now you need to develop a plan together for appropriate action steps and checkpoints to provide coaching and accountability.

1. **Commit to a cadence of 1:1s:** The reason some of the best-laid plans fail is that there is not equal effort invested in executing the plan as there is in formulating the plan. Knowing the plan is not the same as doing the plan. Further, the plan often gets discussed in groups, instead of with individuals. Rarely do people really buy-in in group sessions.

   I believe group meetings are for information and encouragement, but development and correction happen in 1:1s. Here are the steps for effective 1:1s:

   - An initial conversation around how they rate themselves and how you rate them to determine alignment and opportunities.
   - Agreement around your respective roles in the effort. You are the coach, not the boss. This means you are a resource to them. They need to be clear that you will not do the work for them. They need to own the effort and tap into you for assistance and support as needed. You also won't nag, police, or coerce them to do what they agree needs to be done to get where they want to go.
   - Ask the team member what they want to achieve and what their plan is to get there. This is where the S.M.A.R.T. planning approach is helpful—establishing Specific, Measurable, Actionable, Realistic, and Timely plans. They need to tell you their plan and ask you questions about aspects they don't know. Don't tell them what steps they should take, rather draw out

thoughts and ideas. The more you do for them, the less they will do for themselves.

- Once you have agreed on a plan and the relevant action steps, ask them how often they would like to get together to discuss progress. This is where you establish the cadence for your coaching. Some people will need more frequent 1:1s than others. The cadence, or frequency, of your 1:1s will depend on how quickly they can effect change and the timeline for achieving their objective. In the case of a salesperson, who is responsible for monthly production numbers, the cadence probably needs to be weekly. That being said, consistently high producers may only need a single monthly session where they share what their goals are for the month. Your role with them is to encourage them more and support that development. With others who need more development, the cadence may be twice a week. Either way, let the team member tell you how often they want to get together, when they want to do the next session, and what they will have accomplished by then.

A quick reminder about lagging and leading indicators of performance. In the sales example above, the lagging indicator is the actual sales that are closed in a specific period, such as one month. The leading indicators are the actions that are being taken that will ultimately lead to closed sales. One of those actions is the number of outbound prospecting calls. Another is the length of time it takes to supply requested information to customers.

Too many managers focus on the lagging indicator, and by the time the lagging metric is available for consideration, too much time has passed to effect necessary change. Further, the manager often doesn't like conflict and avoids having the necessary conversations in a timely manner.

A farmer who waits for his harvest to determine whether he did a good job of farming will be sorely disappointed. The farmer understands it's more important to focus on tilling, fertilizing, planting, and watering in the spring and summer to have a good harvest in the fall.

I once coached a friend on his weight-loss effort. He was inspired by what I had accomplished and asked me to assist him to do something similar. We followed the foregoing steps and agreed that he would send me a weekly text confirming that he was taking the agreed actions and advising his current weight. We further agreed that we would get together once a month for a more in-depth review of how things were progressing, what challenges he was facing, and whether tweaks needed to be made to the agreed plan.

When he practiced intentionality, he made good progress, but when he fell back into his old habits, progress stalled.

1:1s often involve mentorship. Remember, 1:1s are for correction and development. To have effective 1:1s, a degree of relationship needs to be present, or at least the team member needs to feel like the manager cares about them. Hence, it's common that the person conducting the

1:1 also operates as a mentor and that the person being coached feels comfortable being vulnerable with their coach about their concerns and challenges.

2. **Candid Awareness:** In the weight-loss example, a scale can provide very candid awareness of the current weight and whether progress is being made. Often, however, metrics are not as readily available, and the team member will depend on their coach to provide them with feedback [awareness]. This is especially true when somebody wants to make changes to their behavior and lacks the self-awareness to recognize when they fall short.

   It's vitally important that the coach speaks very forthright with the person being coached, while not being negative or belittling.

   Candor is about being open, honest, and helpful. The person being coached needs very clear and candid feedback so they can adjust their actions as necessary to stay on course or to get back on course when they have strayed.

   When getting together in 1:1s, it's important that the team member reports to you how they are progressing. Many managers are too quick to tell the team member how they believe the individual is doing. This is often because the manager has access to the reports. Ideally, however, the manager needs to provide the team member with access to whatever information they need to pull their own reports and manage their own efforts. Your job as the coach is to listen, be supportive, give direction when asked, and provide resources as needed. It's the team member's job to take the necessary [and agreed] action.

3. **Courageous Accountability:** Providing accountability requires more courage than often realized, even when the other person asks for it. Without appropriate accountability, results suffer.

   Few people enjoy conflict and may avoid providing proper accountability. So, a good agreement between the coach and team member up front is critical to make it easier and so both know it will be coming.

   Accountability can be as simple as the weekly text from my weight-loss friend. If weekly is not enough, then a more frequent cadence may be required. If temptations are high, a daily text may be necessary.

   Accountability provides the team member with extra incentive to stay on course rather than having to face their coach knowing they didn't do what they said they would do.

   When it comes to intentionality, remember that the agreed action steps are anticipated to achieve a certain result. From a weight-loss standpoint, my daily target was 1770 net calories. Straying from that target has a direct impact on my ability to hit my goal. In my case, MyFitnessPal® provided me with the daily accountability to stay on course. I could see a report of what my daily caloric intake was along with my caloric burn from exercise. I had the added benefit of sharing my progress with my wife, which was a form of soft accountability. Others, however, may need to formalize their role from an accountability standpoint so neither of you can avoid it, at least not easily.

In Appendix C I've included a sample template for establishing a Team Member Coaching Effort.

The reason most people don't achieve the things they want is because what they are attempting doesn't come naturally, and they are not practicing intentionality. The challenge with intentionality is that it takes commitment and effort, but that's why The Three Intentionalities are so important if you want to achieve better results.

NOTES AND TAKE-AWAYS

INTENTIONALITY ELEMENTS TO IMPLEMENT

BRINGING IT ALL TOGETHER

Remember the three frogs on the log from the Backstory at the beginning of the book? Well, there are now only two left on the log because the one who had previously just made a decision to jump has followed-through with action and jumped! Before he merely had good intentions, but now he proceeded with intentionality.

This is something that true leaders understand...nothing happens until somebody does something! And the role of the leader is to intentionally influence team members to specific and purposeful action to go from where they are today [HERE] to where they collectively want to go [THERE]. That is what leadership and intentionality are all about...helping people and teams achieve their mutual objectives and goals.

The issue is that action takes energy, and when things aren't natural, easy, or desirous, action requires even more energy. Essentially, we are in a constant battle with personal and natural forces, our Elephant, and the 2nd Law of Thermodynamics holding us back from the things we want to achieve.

It's not just inaction that takes us away from better outcomes. It can be doing things that come naturally and seem harmless on the surface, like resting, eating, and playing. These are good things in the right context and in appropriate quantities but can represent negative actions if they are not aligned with our goals and objectives. Consider the following examples:

1. Rest is good, especially to recover after exerting lots of effort. But too much rest interferes with action and causes our muscles to atrophy.
2. Eating is good for replenishing the nutrients and energy that our bodies need for action, but too much food gets stored as fat, which weighs us down and makes action even more difficult. I know this firsthand because I love food, and if my natural desires exceed my intentionality efforts, I would regain the fifty pounds that I lost.
3. Playing is also good for positivity, reducing cortisol, and creating an environment in which our emotional brains are more engaged, but too much play interferes with getting important work done.

In this book, I have unpacked the concept of intentionality and provided you with several tools to help you move in a better and more desired direction–a direction that will enable you to achieve more of the things you want to achieve. And not only in achieving better results but in sustaining them for longer periods.

The Intentionality Model demonstrates how intentionality works to counteract the forces that keep us from desired achievements. It clarifies that, to achieve specific and purposeful goals and objectives, we must take steps that put us on the same trajectory as our goals and objectives. Not just formulating action plans, which are essentially just thoughts, but taking Intentionality Steps. The potential challenge with intentionality is that it involves actions that are as easy to do as not to do. And, since we don't usually see immediate results from our actions, we need to trust the process that our Intentionality Steps [purposeful actions] will take us where we want to go.

THE INTENTIONALITY MODEL

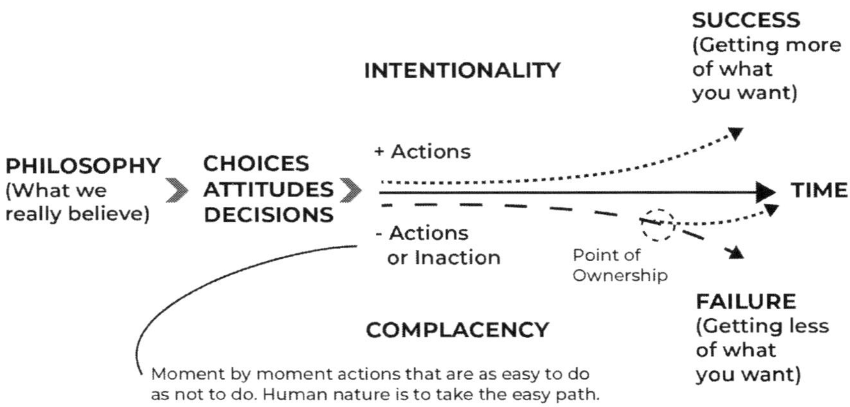

(© Mast 2023)

That is also one of the greatest challenges with leadership. Leadership efforts need to be focused on shaping behaviors, and often the effects of those efforts do not show themselves for weeks, months, and even years. Many of us remember a teacher, coach, or leader who impacted our lives many years ago; how many of us let them know what impact they had? So, in many ways, leadership is a work of faith, trusting that what we are doing is making an impact. This is also why it's so important to work in accordance with timeless principles that we know will make a difference if we just persevere.

Intentionality is also more than just developing good habits, plans, processes, and routines. Each of these can be viewed as intentionality tools.

Intentionality is about taking purposeful action in alignment with one's philosophy. To live with intentionality involves aligning actions with what we really believe, our philosophy of life. While habits, processes, and routines are about doing things consistently, intentionality is about a consistent lifestyle.

For example, if you want to be an athlete, you don't just start each day with a habit of 15 minutes of exercise. Rather, you start living like an athlete, which involves intentionality with the things you eat, the sleep you get, and the other things you do that align with what athletes do.

Or, if you want to retire by a specific age with sufficient funds, you don't just establish a habit of saving. Rather, you set out a plan with Intentionality Steps that will allow you to accumulate specific amounts of money by specific dates. You track progress regularly to ensure your trajectory remains aligned with your targets.

Habits, processes, and routines are important intentionality tools we all need to tap into, especially when attempting things that are not natural for us. By themselves, however, habits, processes, and routines can lack direction and effectiveness. Taken alone habits, processes, and routines would be akin to a train on tracks, where no deviation is possible, while intentionality is akin to a driver following the directions of their GPS system, adjusting as necessary to avoid heavy traffic, for example, or closed roads, or to accommodate important stops along the way.

This is why intentionality is such a powerful mindset for leaders. So much so that I believe it is the missing element, the secret sauce, the magic formula for most people and teams, especially those who struggle to achieve the things they desire.

Armed with an understanding of how intentionality works, the Intentionality Formula provides leaders with a framework to methodically look at any situation, break it down into its elements, and determine where attention needs to be focused and what Intentionality Steps need to be taken with relevant priority.

The Intentionality Formula allows leaders to execute more effective action plans and virtually guarantee results. But you must avoid the fallacy of hope.

THE INTENTIONALITY FORMULA

Results are a direct function of the following inter-related elements:

A. 2 **Executable** 1 **Plan**

\+

B. 4 **Engaged** 3 **Talent**

\+

C. 5 **Commitment** & 6 **Accountability**

\+

D. 7 **Feedback** & 8 **Tweaks**

= X (RESULTS)

(© Mast 2023)

Merriam-Webster defines hope as "a desire accompanied by expectation of or belief in fulfillment". Note, however, there is nothing in the definition that suggests action. That's why hope is not a good strategy. Hope is about desire, expectation, and belief, all of which have disappointed many people when their hopes were not fulfilled. Intentionality is however a good and effective strategy, because of the action it involves.

Consider The Three Intentionalities of a Great Leader, which provides a working model to optimize a leader's greatest resource—the team—recognizing that a highly engaged team can be twice as productive as an unengaged group of people.

To bring it all together, I want to end with one more model that shows how great leadership ultimately translates into better results.

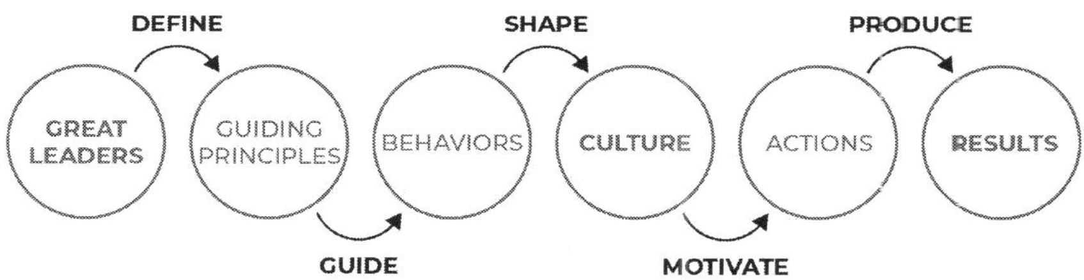

There is a link between a leadership approach with intentionality and better results. Great leaders define the principles that guide the behaviors of team members. These principles include the vision, mission, and values of the organization, along with any other helpful directives that establish the philosophy by which the organization is to operate. It's critical that leaders only hire team members who align with this philosophy; otherwise, incongruent behaviors will be infused into the team, dilute culture, divert actions, and adversely impact results.

Henry Cloud, clinical psychologist, and author of *Boundaries for Leaders*, emphasizes that leaders always get two things: what they create and what they tolerate. Leaders either define [create] clear guiding principles that lead to aligned behaviors and a strong culture or allow [tolerate] ambiguity, which leads to confusion and a weak culture, unengaged team members, and poor results.

Great leaders understand that culture is a powerful tool to attract the right people and repel the wrong ones. A strong culture motivates consistent and purposeful action that produces superior results.

Armed with the foregoing insights and tools, you are not only able to achieve greater results as a team, but you are now able to tackle some of the goals that you have not had the courage, confidence, and motivation to tackle previously.

So, the next time you consider a goal, plan, or objective, don't just talk about it. Rather, formulate Intentionality Steps that will take you where you want to go. Then, moment by moment, day by day, week by week, month by month, year by year, simply follow those Intentionality Steps, and you will get to your goal, plan, or objective…guaranteed!

And, if you need an additional reminder to practice intentionality daily, moment by moment, get yourself an Intentionality Penny or two. I put one in my pocket every morning to remind me to do the little things that are as easy to do as they are not to do. This reminder in many cases has nudged me over the threshold of reluctance that we all face to do that small thing in line with my philosophy and takes me one step closer to my goals and objectives. Because it has a hole in the middle and is a representation of the two key parts of the brain, the Intentionality Penny also reminds me that feelings drive three times more behavior than rational things like money. For leaders, this is an important reminder that, while people need money (the outer part of the penny), money is just a means to an emotional end; money is not the end all. It's one of the leader's greatest opportunities to shape behavior by filling the missing emotional middle of the penny.

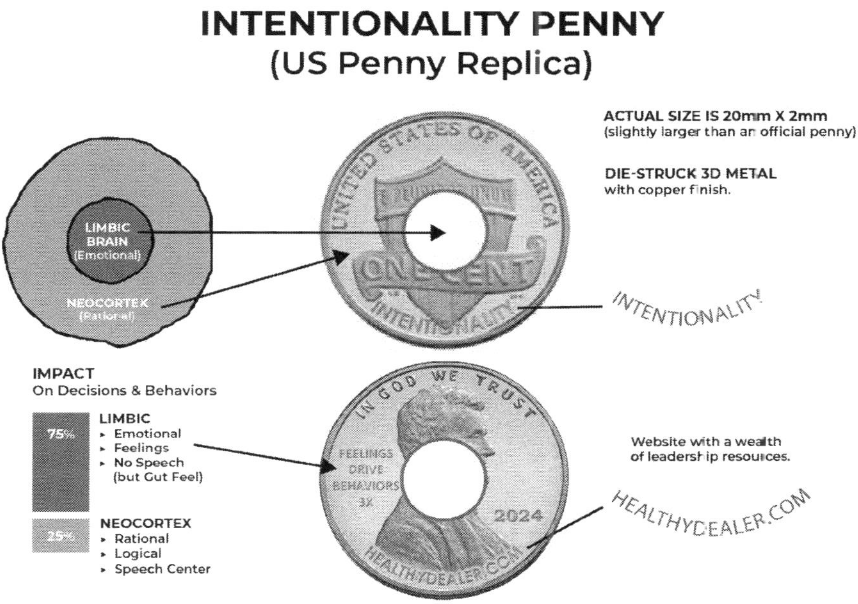

To get an intentionality penny or two for yourself, click on this QR code:

Enjoy the intentionality journey!

APPENDICES

APPENDIX A: WRITING YOUR PHILOSOPHY

Examples of Philosophies:

Epictetus:

- The essence of philosophy is that a man should so live that his happiness shall depend as little as possible on external things.

Aristotle:

- I have gained this from philosophy: that I do without being commanded what others do only from fear of the law.

Eleanor Roosevelt:

- One's philosophy is not best expressed in words; it is expressed in the choices one makes… and the choices we make are ultimately our responsibility.

Steve Jobs:

- The only way to do great work is to do what you love to do.
- Your time is limited; don't waste it living someone else's life.

Alice Roosevelt Longworth:

- I have a simple philosophy: Fill what's empty. Empty what's full. Scratch where it itches.

Theodore Roosevelt:

- Believe you can and you're halfway there.
- Do what you can, with what you have, where you are.

Mahatma Gandhi:

- Be the change you want to see in the world.

Albert Einstein:

- If you want to live a happy life, tie it to a goal, not to people or things.

Mae West:

- You only live once, but if you do it right, once is enough.

Ralph Waldo Emerson:

- What lies behind us and what lies before us are tiny matters compared to what lies within us.

Oscar Wilde:

- Be yourself; everyone else is already taken.

Mark Twain:

- Truth is stranger than fiction, because fiction has to be possible and truth doesn't.

The Golden Rule:

- Treat others the way you want to be treated.

Personal Philosophies: Definition, Steps, and Examples

(The following is from Indeed.com, which at the time of printing was the #1 job site in the world with more than 300M unique visitors each month.)

Developing a personal philosophy, knowing how to define a goal, and discovering your character traits are all critical components to growing and maximizing your career potential. A personal philosophy may help you identify your beliefs and ambitions and ease your decision-making processes. Understanding and adopting a personal philosophy may help you achieve your personal career goals. In this article, we define personal philosophies, outline the steps and tips you can take to craft one, and provide examples.

What are personal philosophies?

Personal philosophies are a collection of guiding concepts that people follow in their daily lives. They can affect the words you speak, the actions you conduct, and the products you buy at a shop. Individuals conceptualize ideologies in a variety of ways. The purpose of these philosophies is to establish an alignment between your ideas, words, and deeds that is genuine to you and helps you achieve your personal and professional goals.

Your personal philosophies encompass your beliefs, priorities, and expectations. You can usually state your philosophies and principles in a brief sentence. Personal principles are unique to each individual. The following are the four important components of your own philosophy:

Theory: This pertains to your views and ideas on your guiding principles.

Attitude: Your attitude encompasses your feelings and describes how you act on those feelings.

Guiding principles: These are your personal views and ideas that you use when making life choices.

Behavior: Your behavior relates to how you conduct yourself.

What is the significance of personal philosophy?

A personal philosophy is significant because it may serve as a decision-making guideline for how you spend your time, connect with people, and do your work.

Here are three advantages of developing a personal leadership philosophy:

Ensures consistency: You're more likely to be consistent with your actions and behaviors if you have a personal philosophy.

Helps you understand your character: Having a personal leadership philosophy can help you understand your character. This is significant because your personality influences how you interact with others and in various settings.

Encourages meaningful cooperation: This style of thought encourages meaningful collaboration. When your colleagues understand why you act the way you do, they're more likely to cooperate with you since they're aware of and at ease with your leadership style.

How to create your own philosophy:

Consider the following stages while developing a personal philosophy:

1. **Think about what you value**

   Before you start creating your own philosophy, it's important that you think about what values you believe make a strong individual. These are the values that you may emphasize in your philosophy. When it comes to your conduct, it's equally crucial to identify your strengths and values. Concentrate on the precise ideals that help you become a better leader and impact your decisions. Make a note of your previous successes and failures if it helps. This is going to assist you in defining your values and your priorities.

2. **Establish your objectives**

   When developing your own philosophy, think about what you want to achieve and what results you want to see. Determine how you would attain these goals, what they may accomplish, and how long it would take you to achieve these goals. Consider how the values you choose in the previous stage can help you achieve or affect these objectives.

3. **Seek mentorship**

Inquire about the personal philosophy of a leader or an industry expert you appreciate. Discuss your basic values with a personal or business mentor. Look up to the individuals you admire to help you develop your philosophy. Consider incorporating a couple of their objectives, tactics, or procedures into your philosophy. Make a note of any values or objectives with which you have a strong connection and add them to your lists from stages one and two.

4. **Reflect on the impact you want to make**

Consider the impact you want to make on the world and how your skill set is going to enable you to do so. To start drafting your philosophy, consider the following questions:

- *What do you aim to produce, modify, or preserve in the long run?*
- *How exactly do you want to change the world when you leave it?*
- *Who and how do you wish to help using your particular talents and abilities?*
- *Which knowledge base or skill set can assist you in achieving your goals?*
- *What do you believe your goal to be?*
- *What distinguishing skills, talents, abilities, and characteristics do you offer?*
- *What is it about a purpose or a vision that motivates you?*

5. **Begin developing your philosophy**

Examine your list of values and objectives. Emphasize the most crucial aim. Then, underline the value that can have the most influence on accomplishing that objective. To help you focus on your most essential ideals and ambitions, consider the following list of sentence starters:

- *I always...*
- *I devote time to...*
- *I appreciate...*
- *I'm fascinated about...*
- *I admire...*
- *I care about...*
- *I am listening with...*
- *I inspire to...*

After that, start formulating your personal philosophy. Create a brief and straightforward statement that covers both the emphasized aim and value from step four. Some personal principles are as short as one sentence. Others are a list of bullet points that express objectives, values, and expectations. Some of the paragraphs are brief. Revise your own leadership philosophy until you discover the perfect phrase for you. Writing your philosophy can help you organize your thoughts and guarantee that you say what you want to say. This can also hold you accountable.

6. **Think about your philosophy**

   After you've created your own philosophy, assess how well you've adhered to it over time. If you don't feel like you've been acting or behaving in accordance with your philosophy, let it guide you back to becoming the person you want to be. Consider the acts you've performed that have deviated from your philosophy and which you've stuck to. Finally, reflecting on your philosophy can help you discover areas where you can improve or elements of your philosophy that are no longer achievable.

Tips for creating a personal philosophy:

Here are a few more tips to help you craft an effective personal purpose statement.

- ***Be honest with yourself:*** *Your personal philosophy is to represent your biggest passion and your long-term goal. Recognize that it's good to revise your mission statement as you develop and learn.*
- ***Keep it brief:*** *As the goal is to concentrate solely on what is most important, your personal philosophy is to be no more than one phrase in length. Try jotting down five words that characterize you and your mission to help you discover that one item and narrow it down to two words that characterize you and your purpose from the list of five words.*

- ***Obtain feedback:*** *Communicate your own stated purpose with the individuals that matter the most in your life. They can supply you with valuable information that allows you to enhance the statement.*

Outlined below are some examples of philosophies you may consider:

1. Failures are lessons to learn from.

   This philosophy centers on tenacity. It essentially suggests that you keep moving towards your objective and take action to get closer to it, no matter what challenges you encounter. If this is your philosophy, you understand that every failure is only a consequence from which you may learn, and you may approach setbacks with a development mentality to find the lesson. You consider what went wrong or what you can do differently the next time.

2. I don't have to understand everything all the time.

   If this is your personal philosophy, you may be more willing to grow and learn new things. For example, you might be more comfortable completing new tasks or taking on new roles. If this is your philosophy, you may work to study and expand your knowledge.

3. I base my action on my integrity.

   When you conduct with integrity, you act in accordance with your principles. Working against your values jeopardizes your integrity. People can know what to anticipate from you if you commit to always operating with honesty. They can put their faith in you to act in a way that matches your moral code.

APPENDIX B: CALCULATIONS

Compound interest is the **eighth wonder of the world**. *He who understands it, earns it… he who doesn't… pays it.*

— ALBERT EINSTEIN

Here is the math showing how one penny can become over a billion pennies in just a matter of 30 days:

	Start with	Add	Total
Day 1	$ 0.01	$ 0.01	$ 0.02
Day 2	$ 0.02	$ 0.02	$ 0.04
Day 3	$ 0.04	$ 0.04	$ 0.08
Day 4	$ 0.08	$ 0.08	$ 0.16
Day 5	$ 0.16	$ 0.16	$ 0.32
Day 6	$ 0.32	$ 0.32	$ 0.64
Day 7	$ 0.64	$ 0.64	$ 1.28
Day 8	$ 1.28	$ 1.28	$ 2.56
Day 9	$ 2.56	$ 2.56	$ 5.12
Day 10	$ 5.12	$ 5.12	$ 10.24
Day 11	$ 10.24	$ 10.24	$ 20.48
Day 12	$ 20.48	$ 20.48	$ 40.96
Day 13	$ 40.96	$ 40.96	$ 81.92
Day 14	$ 81.92	$ 81.92	$ 163.84
Day 15	$ 163.84	$ 163.84	$ 327.68
Day 16	$ 327.68	$ 327.68	$ 655.36
Day 17	$ 655.36	$ 655.36	$ 1,310.72
Day 18	$ 1,310.72	$ 1,310.72	$ 2,621.44
Day 19	$ 2,621.44	$ 2,621.44	$ 5,242.88
Day 20	$ 5,242.88	$ 5,242.88	$ 10,485.76
Day 21	$ 10,485.76	$ 10,485.76	$ 20,971.52
Day 22	$ 20,971.52	$ 20,971.52	$ 41,943.04
Day 23	$ 41,943.04	$ 41,943.04	$ 83,886.08
Day 24	$ 83,886.08	$ 83,886.08	$ 167,772.16
Day 25	$ 167,772.16	$ 167,772.16	$ 335,544.32
Day 26	$ 335,544.32	$ 335,544.32	$ 671,088.64
Day 27	$ 671,088.64	$ 671,088.64	$ 1,342,177.28
Day 28	$ 1,342,177.28	$ 1,342,177.28	$ 2,684,354.56
Day 29	$ 2,684,354.56	$ 2,684,354.56	$ 5,368,709.12
Day 30	$ 5,368,709.12	$ 5,368,709.12	$ 10,737,418.24

APPENDIX C: TEAM MEMBER COACHING EFFORTS

A high resolution pdf can also be downloaded from http://healthydealer.com/intentionality-for-leaders/

1:1 Session conducted by ______________ with ______________ Date _______/___

Coaching Team Members to Become Their Best. Follow these steps:

1. **Take Inventory: (1-10)** **Current** — Their Best / Potential: **My View** **Their View**
   (Assign rating on each element below)

	Current	My View	Their View
• **Capable:**			
o **Ability**	______	______	______
o **Capacity**	______	______	______
• **Cohesive:**			
o **Aligned**	______	______	______
o **Trustworthiness**	______	______	______
• **Hungry:**			
o **Desire**	______	______	______
o **Effort**	______	______	______
• **Performance on Key Metric(s):**			
o __________	______	______	______
o __________	______	______	______
o __________	______	______	______

2. **Do they agree their potential is higher than current performance?** Y N

3. **Do they desire to improve performance?** Y N

4. **Do they desire coaching/assistance?** Y N

5. **What do they feel our 1:1 Cadence should be?:**

   Frequency ____________ When will we meet next ___________/_____

6. **What Intentionality Steps do they propose? (Specific, time frame, metrics)**

7. **What support do they want from me (leader/coach)?**

ACKNOWLEDGMENTS

There are so many people that I need and would like to thank for having influenced and inspired me and my development, but it's impossible to recollect everybody and all that they did. In some way or another, every person that crosses our path influences us in some way. Their core contribution is often as simple as the awareness (often initially viewed as criticism) they provide, for without awareness, our development would be stunted. In other ways, they provide accountability to stay the course of our commitments. And probably the biggest impact was made by the encouragement they provided. Whether awareness, accountability, or encouragement, all are important elements of coaching as we strive to become our best. So, whether directly or indirectly, we all have the power to develop the potential in others. This is what Henry Cloud communicates in his book, *The Power of the Other*.

I'm glad that I heard early in my career that *leaders are readers*. Sadly, according to an article by Mental Floss, *Who Reads Books?*, here are a few surprising statistics from a 2003 survey conducted by an organization called the Jenkins Group:

- 33% of high school graduates never read another book for the rest of their lives.

- 42% of college graduates never read another book after college.
- 80% of U.S. families did not buy or read a book last year.

Hopefully, some things have changed since 2003. Unfortunately, unless society has adopted greater intentionality since then, the numbers are probably the same or worse. Thankfully, I read a business magazine article on leaders being readers in the early 1990s, which put me on a path of reading. Three of the ten business executives interviewed for the article suggested that Stephen R. Covey's *The Seven Habits of Highly Effective People* was the most impactful book they had read. As I researched the book, I discovered that it was a National Bestseller, so that's the book I started with.

The first principle in Covey's book is to *Be Proactive*. Reading provides awareness and represents a proactive investment in one's future. Reading, like many other forms of learning, provides many of the building blocks that we rely on later in our careers and life but won't be available to us if we don't proactively invest. You can't build a house with the wood from the seedlings planted today. Knowledge and wisdom are like trees: they take years to grow.

Another book that significantly influenced my leadership and coaching early on was *The Five Temptations of a CEO* by Patrick Lencioni. It was given to me by a business associate at a pivotal time in my career. I was just embarking on a new venture, this time in the software industry. It was Pat's first book, and I devoured it. I love Pat's writing style, usually in the form of a fable to make the principles relatable and followed by a summary of the principles presented. From that time forward, Pat became a mentor to me, albeit unbeknownst to him, as I read every book he published, including: *The Five Dysfunctions of a Team*, *Death by Meeting*, *The*

Advantage, *The Motive*, *Getting Naked*, and *The Ideal Team Player*, amongst others.

I had the privilege of meeting Pat, along with Jeff Gibson, his President of Consulting, in 2015. Pat has challenged me in many positive ways and influenced my career path more than he knows. I 'm thankful to Pat for providing me with an understanding of Organizational Health. I use his models and tools extensively in my coaching because they provide a simple and effective way of implementing powerful principles and concepts that can have a huge impact on leaders and teams. He also challenged me with regards to another book he said I should write, specific to the Auto Industry…a book I've started writing. Stay tuned.

A few of the other authors I would like to give special mention to for the role they have played in my development are:

Henry Cloud, speaker, and author of many powerful leadership books, including *Boundaries for Leaders*, *Necessary Endings*, and *The Power of the Other.* I love all of his books and find them not only insightful but enjoyable to read. Dr. Cloud has an incredible way of sharing powerful perspectives that are helpful for individuals, couples, and leaders. He is also a clinical psychologist and executive coach, who writes extensively about neuroscience. He has helped me in so many ways, especially the role of the brain as it relates to intentionality, leadership, and relationships in general. I had the privilege of meeting Henry years ago. My wife also benefited greatly from his *Boundaries* book many years ago and currently subscribes to Dr. Cloud's boundaries.me for daily encouragement and reinforcement of healthy perspectives.

Simon Sinek, speaker and author of many leadership books, including *Start with Why*, *Leaders Eat Last*, and *The Infinite Game.* Sinek's *Golden Circle* has been very helpful in connecting the dots between leadership and neuroscience. Simon and I are incredibly aligned when it comes to leadership and building a more engaging and fulfilling work environment.

Brene Brown, speaker, storyteller, and author of many leadership books, including *Daring Greatly*, *Braving the Wilderness*, and *Dare to Lead*. I have learned so much from Brene about the role of shame, blame, and vulnerability in leadership. Thank you, Brene, for daring greatly in the writing of your books and the courageous talks that you give.

Some of the many other authors that I want to acknowledge are:

- Kevin Leman - *The Way of the Shepherd*
- James Hunter - *The Servant*
- Carmine Gallo - *The Storyteller's Secret*
- Dan and Chip Heath - *Switch*
- Jim Collins - *Good to Great*
- Shawn Achor - *The Happiness Advantage*
- Liz Wiseman - *Multipliers*
- Marshall Goldsmith - *What Got You Here Won't Get You There*
- Geoffrey A. Moore - *Crossing The Chasm*
- Jocko Willink and Leif Babin - *Extreme Ownership*
- Daniel H. Pink - *Drive*
- Kim Scott - *Radical Candor*
- Mark Batterson - *Win The Day*
- Joshua Metcalf - *Burn Your Goals*
- And many others

Writing a book is ultimately an act of love. It requires passion to write for hundreds of hours not knowing what impact the effort will make. The writer gives of themselves, not only in hours of time but in vulnerability of soul, in a selfless manner for the betterment of others. I'm thankful to the many authors who have given of themselves so I could grow as a person, leader, and coach.

In 2009, I had the opportunity to get involved with the automotive industry. Like most consumers, I had a very tainted view of car dealerships and could never have imagined working in the industry. But, after selling one of my companies, I was invited to lead a car dealership. It was a huge learning curve. In May 2010, I had the privilege of attending a Ford Dealer meeting in Dearborn, Michigan. Amongst the many other things that took place during that event, I will never forget a couple of them. The first took place when Alan Mulally took the stage to speak to the thousands of Dealers and General Managers who had gathered to hear Ford Executives reveal strategies, tactics, and products for the following year. Typically, each Ford Executive had a well-scripted PowerPoint presentation that supported the message they shared with the audience, along with their message displayed on a teleprompter.

When Alan Mulally took the stage, however, something very intriguing happened…all the screens and teleprompters turned off, and Alan delivered a powerful message from the heart. The room was silent, and everybody was focused on Alan and the vision he was sharing. It was a powerful presentation.

The second took place in the evening reception. Everybody was mingling, and there was a curious roped-off area where something was being set up. Alan Mulally was there, so I was curious what was going to take place. The next thing I knew, Alan walked over to me and said, "You can be first" as he invited me inside the ropes. It turns out the area was set up so that Dealers and General Managers could get their picture taken with Alan as a keepsake of the event. At Alan's invitation, I was the first to get my picture with him. That was cool! That picture with Alan has been the main screen on my phone for more than ten years because it was a picture with Alan Mulally and because it was prior to my losing fifty pounds, and it serves as a daily reminder of a physical state I don't want to backslide into.

In 2011, through the inspiration of Alan Mulally and the influence of Dr. Harry Cohen [and others], Ford Motor Company developed an initiative where they engaged leadership coaches to work with their 3,000+ stores to improve the customer experience. It was Alan Mulally's speech at a Dealer Meeting in Dearborn that inspired me to join the effort. For more than ten years, I had the privilege of coaching Ford Dealers and their teams across the nation. I had the opportunity to meet Alan on a couple of occasions. Alan is an incredibly principle-centered leader who has hugely impacted my coaching, and I regularly refer to things he said and did. He demonstrated that leadership principles transcend industry, and I'm confident that, with intentionality, we can overcome the negative stigma the automotive industry has earned over the last century. Thank you, Alan, for your inspiration.

Ford's Consumer Experience Movement (CEM) was a great incubator for me as I further developed my coaching skills. I met many wonderful people within the ranks of Ford Motor Company, Ford and Lincoln Dealerships, Coaching Companies that ultimately executed the vision, and fellow coaches who took the vision to the front lines in a very missional manner. During that time, I had the privilege of getting to know Dr. Harry Cohen–psychologist, speaker, author, and executive coach. He was at the grassroots giving life to CEM, XL2000, and many other Ford initiatives for 20+ years that continue to impact the way the Ford community leads and serves. In Harry's book, *Be The Sun…Not The Salt*, he translates the heliotropic effect, the tendency of living organisms to turn toward the sun [life-giving sources] into human terms. This book is the personification of Harry and the way he strives to live.

Harry once shared a simple and profound perspective with me when he said, "It's better to be helpful than right." Thanks, Harry, this perspective has helped me navigate a number of sensitive conversations.

Thanks also, Harry, for agreeing to write the forward to this book. You not only understand the principles and perspectives I present in this book, but you have journeyed with me over the past decade and have helped to shape me as a coach. I will be forever grateful for your influence and inspiration.

I'm thankful to my parents, who not only gave me life, but encouraged me throughout my life, and provided me with endless opportunities for development. One of those opportunities was to work in one of their companies. I learned the value of hard work at a young age. My parents periodically retell the story of how I developed math skills at the age of five by collecting discarded pop bottles and cashing them in at the local store for a nickel a piece. At six, I earned $0.25/hr. sweeping floors in my father's warehouse. Over the ensuing fifteen years, I developed skills that eventually allowed me to work my way through college and pay for my own tuition, graduating without student debt. My parents trusted me with greater and greater responsibility and gave me opportunities that allowed me to develop some of my first business and leadership skills.

I'm thankful for the many educators, coaches, pastors, and camp counselors who not only imparted knowledge to me in the classroom and on the sports field but for those times when they taught me valuable life lessons informally. One of those teachers was Mrs. Reagan in fourth grade. She identified something in me at an early age, which I only started to understand and appreciate later in life. I was an active child and was always stirring things up with fellow classmates. During one of those times, she came close to me, looked deep into my eyes, and said with a stern voice as she pointed her finger at me, "You're an instigator." She identified a natural element in my personality that plays an important role in my coaching and leading, the art of being candid, having difficult conversations, and telling the kind truth. I don't think Mrs. Reagan meant it that way at the time, but I'm thankful for the awareness she provided, nonetheless.

I'm thankful to my many clients who have trusted me to coach them and their team members. In the process, I have also built many lifelong friendships. The work of a leadership coach involves many privileged sessions where I can not reveal to the person signing my check what their team member and I talked about. In the process, however, I was able to guide the thoughts and actions of both the team member and their leader toward a better mutual result. One of my clients seemed to sum it up best when somebody asked him why he invited me to spend time with his team monthly over many years, when he said, "There's no place on the financial statement that shows the impact Herb has made, but Herb brings a different element than I do, and I can tell you my team communicates better and works together better as a result!"

A huge shout-out goes to my wife of more than forty years. For her unyielding support and loving partnership throughout our many endeavors. We not only do life together, have raised three fantastic children who are now, in turn, adding to our quiver of grandchildren, but have built several companies together. It's been quite a ride, and there's nobody I would rather journey with!

And, most importantly, I thank God who gives me life and breath and grace. He decided what DNA I should have and then directed my steps over more than half a century, through the highs and lows, to shape me into the person I am today…and He's not done with me yet. He is my source of strength but doesn't impose Himself on me. He makes Himself available when I'm ready as I've learned here too that my natural tendencies are to try to do things with my own strength. So, as with so many other areas, I practice intentionality daily to tap into His strength, which is so much greater than anything I could ever muster or imagine.

ABOUT THE AUTHOR

Herb is the founder and CEO of HealthyDealer, a leadership development organization. Herb envisions a world in which people go to work inspired, are coached in a positive, safe, and supportive environment to be their best, and go home at the end of day with a feeling of fulfillment for the contributions they have made in furthering the vision and mission of the organization. Realizing this vision becomes possible when our organizations are run by leaders who operate with intentionality. Herb is best described as a "gap-filler" and "dot-connector" as he helps leaders better understand the things they don't yet know and how the things they already know fit together to become better leaders. His efforts are largely focused on developing leaders because he believes the other essential elements of successful organizations, like teamwork, culture, communication, and organizational health, are byproducts of great leadership. The first half of Herb's career was focused on developing his own leadership skills through founding and growing multiple companies. The second half is devoted to developing leaders and helping people, teams, and leaders achieve greater success through a practice of intentionality. When he's not traveling for business, coaching clients, and/or speaking about leadership, organizational health, and intentionality, you can often find Herb enjoying time with his wife or chasing a little ball around the golf course. Herb lives with his wife of forty years, Jocelyn, in the Midwest. Together, they enjoy their three children and spouses and six grandchildren.

Herb K. Mast, Founder and CEO
Cohesion, Inc dba HealthyDealer
Website: HealthyDealer.com
Email: hkmast@healthydealer.com

ABOUT THE COMPANY

Cohesion, Inc is a leadership development organization headquartered in Lincoln, NE. Founded in 2012, the organization represents a culmination of more than twenty-five years of hands-on leadership by Herb in a number of innovative companies, many of which he founded, across a number of different industries. Herb believes employees and customers, while central to a thriving business, are often neglected. Knowing is not the same as doing. Many bosses talk the talk but struggle in executing what they know they should do. The challenge lies in an underdeveloped understanding of, and skill in, leading people, building a healthy organization, and operating with intentionality.

Cohesion, Inc dba HealthyDealer
Website: HealthyDealer.com
Email: hkmast@healthydealer.com

Made in the USA
Columbia, SC
23 November 2023

9bd301b8-b625-4902-b90f-3e74dfbb9d05R01